최원철 시집
The Collection of Won Chul Choi's Poems
한영대역판
Korean-English Translation

붓꽃으로 다가온 당신

You Who came to Me as an Iris

우전(雨田) 최 원 철
Won Chul Choi, Dr.rer.nat.
(Pseudonym : Rain-Blessed Field)

다솜출판사

시인의 말

아침에 눈을 뜨면 불안이 먼저 찾아옵니다. 코로나바이러스 19에 대한 양성인 사람들과 사망자가 늘어나는 소식이 우리를 슬프게 만들게 합니다. 많은 전염병 중에서 흑사병, 천연두, 결핵, 콜레라, 황열병, 독감 등이 일어날 때마다 원인을 인간의 타락이나 전쟁에서 찾을 수도 있습니다. 전염병이 한 국가를 망하게 하고 시대적으로 사상과 습관을 바꿔 놓기도 합니다. 지금 이 시점이 다시 불확실성의 시대로 회귀하고 있음을 알 수 있습니다.

의료진의 영웅적인 헌신이 있으므로 우리의 생명이 연장되기도 합니다. 이러한 사건을 볼 때 문학인들이 가만히 지켜볼 수 없습니다. 우리에게는 마음과 육체의 평안함이 필요한 때입니다. 필자는 우리의 애절한 호소를 신神에게 기도하기도 하고 삶의 노래도 불러야 하겠다는 생각에서 한 편의 시詩를 쓰고 싶었습니다. 물론 이것에 모든 목적을 두고 시詩를 쓰려는 것은 아닙니다. 우리의 삶을 윤택하게 하는 데에 도움이 될 한 편의 시詩가 있다면 행복할 것입니다. 영혼의 문제는 성직자들의 몫이고 시인은 오로지 들리지 않는 마음속의 노래라도 부를 수 있다면 충분하다고 생각합니다. 『붓꽃으로 다가온 당신』이라는 제목으로 시집을 내놓게 되었습니다. 한편의 시詩를 읽더라도 마음의 평안을 느낄 수 있다면 필자는 행복할 것입니다.

감사합니다.

Remark of the poet

When I open my eyes in the morning, anxiety comes first. The news of an increasing number of COVID-19 positive people and deaths is making us sad. Among many infectious diseases, black death, smallpox, tuberculosis, cholera, yellow fever, flu, etc. could be found to have been caused by human corruption or war. Infectious diseases sometimes have ruined a country or changed ideas and habits of the times. This time point of now cannot but be a turning point for returning to an era of uncertainty.

The heroic dedication of the medical staff sometimes extends our lives. When looking at such an event, even literary men cannot just keep watching quietly. It is time when we need peace of mind and body. Therefore, I wanted to at least write a poem with the thought that I should pray to God for our sorrowful appeals and sing songs of life. Of course, this does not mean that this is the entire purpose of writing poets. We will be happy if we have at least a poem that helps enrich our lives. The problems of the soul are something that can be taken care of by the clergy, and I think that if poets can sing inaudible songs in mind, that will be sufficient for them. This is why I became publish a collection of poetry under the title "You Came to Me as an Iris." I will be just happy if you can feel the peace of mind even through a poem.

Thank you.

차례 Contents

제1장 문을 열수록
Chapter I The More the Door is Opened

제2장 사랑의 미혹迷惑

Chapter Ⅱ The Delusion of Love

제3장
이 애처로운 손을 보시고

Chapter Ⅲ
After Seeing This Pathetic Hand

제4장 붓꽃으로 다가온 당신
Chapter Ⅳ You Who came to Me as an Iris

제5장 참회懺悔의 장

Chapter Ⅴ The Penitentiary Chapter

제1장 문을 열수록

Chapter I
The More the Door is Opened

그대의 호수

시간이 멈추어 선 호수 속을 들여다본다
나를 품에 안고 있다

한여름 잠자리가 꼬리로 자맥질하던 흔적
물노린재가 스케이트 타다 미끄러진 표면은 유리 같다

끊임없이 출렁이는 시간 사이에
위선의 베일을 쓴 탈색된 바람이 지나가고
영원의 별빛이 쏟아져 내리기도 한다

창 넘어 들어오는 별빛은
마음 깊은 곳으로 스며들지만
욕망의 파도는 일어나지 않는다
사랑이 심장의 고동 소리를 높이고
눈썹 위에 앉은 졸음은 길을 잃는다

서툴고 위태한 숨결로써
변질된 순금을 추구하는 젊은이들과
누런 구리가 되어버린 노인들의 잃어버린 금빛을
미적분微積分하여 산출된 방정식은
잔잔하게 파문 이는 호수 위에 나래를 펴는 사랑이다
푸른 호수에는 각종 생명이 돋아나기 시작한다
창조자는 빙그레 웃으며 쳐다보고만 있다

Your Lake

I look into the lake where time stopped
It is holding me in its arms

The traces of dragonflies dipping their tails in the height of summer
The surface where stink bugs slipped while skating is like glass.

Between the times that constantly fluctuate
The bleached wind wearing a veil of hypocrisy passes
Eternal starlight pours down sometimes.

The starlight coming through the window
Penetrates deep into my heart
But waves of desire do not arise
Love raises the beat of the heart
The sleepiness sitting on the eyebrows gets lost

The equation produced through differential and integral calculus
Of young people who are pursuing denatured pure gold
With clumsy and precarious waves of breath and
The lost gold color of the elderly who became yellow copper
Is the love that spreads wings over the lake where gentle ripples arise
Various lives begin to sprout in the blue lake.
The creator is just looking at them while smiling

별빛은
호수에 내리지만
한없이 깊고 맑은 소녀의 눈동자가 사라져도
하늘에 더 높은 그리움이 솟구친다

붓끝은 그대 호수에서 생명을 이어가고 있다

Although starlight
Falls on the lake
Even if the infinitely deep and clear pupils of a girl disappear
Higher longing surges to the sky

The tip of the brush carries on life in your lake.

문을 열 수록

자연과학의 문을 열었다
들어갈수록 자연의 섭리가 회진回診하고 있었고
신神의 호흡이 숨 쉬고 있었다

어두움은 호흡을 훔쳐내어
고통의 싹에 덧입혀
씨뿌리는 자의 손에 넘겼다
농부는 씨앗 보관창고를 조심스레 열고
숨소리 죽여가며 호기심과 기쁨을 씨앗에 버무린다

가쁜 호흡을 내 쉬는 밭도 즐거워한다
요즘 와서는
진정한 호흡에 쾌락만 덩그러니 허공에 떠돌고
발아가 별로 중요치 않다

문을 열 때마다 판도라 상자에는
삶의 윤리가 변질하고
암세포며 바이러스가 눈을 뜨고 빤히 쳐다본다

플라스크 안에 가두고 키웠다
자유가 제한을 받자 증오를 품은 죽음이 눈을 부라린다
섬뜩한 마음이 호흡을 멈추게 한다

The More the Door is Opened

The door of natural science was opened
As we entered further, the providence of nature was turning round
And the breathing of God continued

The darkness stole the breath
Overlaid it on the buds of pain
And handed over the buds to the sower
The farmer carefully opened the seed warehouse
And mixed curiosity and joy into seeds while holding his breath

The field gasping for breath is also delighted
These days
With true breath, only pleasure is floating in the air, and
Germination is not very important

Every time the door is opened, in the Pandora box
The ethics of life is spoiled
Cancer cells and viruses open their eyes and stare

Trapped in a flask and raised
When freedom is limited, the angry death glares.
The frightened heart stops breathing

하나의 문을 지나면
또 다른 문이 기다리고 있어
과학은 신神의 비밀의 문을 열기에 바쁘고
나타나는 어긋진 운명만 피곤타

자만自慢에 가득한 과학으로
하늘 문이 닫힐까 두렵다

When one door has been passed
Another door is waiting
Science is busy opening the secret door of God
Only the misaligned fate that appears is tired

With a science full of conceit
I am afraid that the door of heaven will be closed

새해의 기도

옛 껍질을 벗는
누에나, 매미 같은 곤충들과,
수많은 동물도 허물 벗는 것을 보았습니다
2020번의 새해가 다가와도
나는
단 한 번의 탈피를 해본 적이 없습니다

고정된 사고방식이나 집착에서 탈피 못 하고
자신 속에 매몰되면
옛 껍질에 갇혀 죽게 된다는 것을 이제야 알았습니다

이전以前 것은 지나고 새것이 열리는 순간
과거에 매이면 미래를 볼 수 없음도 깨달았습니다
새해엔
옛것을 벗고 새로운 피조물로
당신의 나라에 일원이 되기를 원합니다
당신이
다시 새해의 문을 열고
닫는 일 계속할 동안
나의 문이 닫히는 그 날까지
이웃을 위한 어진 손이 되어 살고 싶습니다

Prayer of the New Year

I have seen
Insects like silkworms and cicadas, and
Numerous animals slipping out of their old skin
Despite that a new year came 2020 times
I have never slip out of my skin even once

The fact that if one fail to slip out of a fixed way of thinking or obsession
And is buried in himself/herself
He/she will die trapped in the old shell has not been understood until now.

The fact that at the moment when the previous one passed and the new one opens
If one is was tied to the past, he/she cannot see the future was also realized.
In the new year
I want to slip out of old things, and as a new creation,
Become a member of your country
While you
Continue to open and close
the of New Year
While the closing day continues
Until the day my door is closed
I want to live as a benevolent hand for my neighbors

별을 보며

마음을 모으고 눈을 감아 보세요
기쁨으로 만난 그대
근심의 눈물 멈추고
하늘에서 내린 기적 생각나지 않나요?

눈을 감고 조용히 두 손 모아보세요
헝클어진 마음 추스르며 기댄 가슴
영원히 동행하자던 언약 기억나지 않나요?

두 손을 귀에 대고 조용히 들어보세요
외로움에 이어진 그리움의 끈을
놓지 못한 채
아직도 심장 뛰는 소리가 들리고 있군요

견딜 수 없는 눈물과 괴로움일 랑
별빛으로 씻으며
봐도 봐도 못 난 당신을 그리워합니다

Looking at the Stars

Collect your mind and close your eyes
You, whom I met with joy
Stop the tears of worries
Don't you remember the miracle granted by the sky?

Close your eyes and quietly put your hands together
Don't you remember the heart you leaned on when you were getting your tangled mind together
And the covenant to accompany forever?

Put your hands on your ears and listen quietly
Without releasing
The string of longing that leads to loneliness
The sound of heart beating is still heard

Washing the unbearable tears and pain
With starlight
I miss you, who is foolish no matter how many times I see you

별빛 내리는 언덕에서

슬픈 멍에에 메일 때
별빛 내리는 언덕에 올라 밤하늘을 봐요

숨 가쁘게 흩어지는 수많은 유성
어디서부터 어디로 가는지 알 수 없어도
아름다운 빛을 내며 사라지네요

계절 따라 흐르는 별과 별 사이
창조주의 모습이 보이잖아요?

머리 둘 곳 없다던 사람의 아들
세상에 남겨 놓은 영원한 사랑
사라지지 않는 밝은 빛으로
내 마음을 곱게 비추고 있네요

On the Hill Where Starlight Falls

When tied to a sad yoke
I climb up the hill where starlight falls and look at the night sky

Countless meteors that breathless scatter
Although I do not know from where to where they go
They disappear emitting beautiful lights

Between the stars seasonally
The figure of the Creator is seen

The son of a man who said he had no place to put his head
Left eternal love in the world
With a bright light that does not disappear
Illuminates my mind beautifully

원초적 구원

흑암과 혼돈 속에서
신神의 혀에서 나오는 ‘말씀’은
“빛이 있으라” 했으니
모든 생성生成은 혀에서 출발한 셈이다

시간이 기울면
검은 파피루스를 하늘에 편다
나는 작은 촛대에 불을 켜
흑암을 물질로 계산해 본다
빛은 밤의 에너지에서 나오는 파장이기 때문이다

검은 파피루스에 그려진 별들은
물결 위에서 반짝이다 내 마음속으로 들어왔다.
달도 들어왔다.
이때, 낯선 사랑을 알게 되었다

흑암은 빛의 어머니

나도 어둠에서 나온 걸까?
신神은 나를 구하려 흑암 속에 손을 넣어 휘저을 때
소용돌이가 생기고 중력이 높아간 블랙홀에서
나를 끄집어내어 빛의 옷을 입혔음이다

Original Salvation

In dead darkness and chaos
The "words" that from the tongue of God were
"Let there be light", therefore,
All creations began from the tongue.

When time has inclined
Black papyrus is spread in the sky
I light a small candlestick
And calculate dead darkness as matter
Because light is wavelengths coming out from the energy of the night

The stars drawn on the black papyrus
Glittered on the waves and entered my mind.
The moon has also entered.
At that time, I became to know a strange love

Darkness is the mother of light

Have I also come from the dark?
When God put his hand into the dead darkness and stirred it to save me
From the black hole where vortex was formed, and the gravity was hightened
He took me out and put a light robe on me.

나는 눈뜬 소경

모든 것이 어둠에서 태어나도
고귀한 영들은 다시 어둠에 들지 않으려 애를 쓴다
살아있음을 나타내는 증거이기 때문이다

어둠과 밝음을 넘나들며
비에 젖고 햇볕에 그을릴 줄 아는
멀쩡한 '나'라는 인간

어둠이 더 위대한 에너지의 근원이라는 나의 외침을
혐오하는 자들의 거센 반발에
나는 진실에 회색 칠하는
눈뜬 소경으로 살아남는 법을 배운다

어둠 뒤편에서 피어오르는 검은 연기 속
산화 중인 화염의 불길에서 뛰쳐나오려는 저주받은 무리에게
기적은 보이질 않는다

땅에 침을 뱉어 진흙을 이겨 눈에 발라주고
못에 가서 씻으라는 권유
언어의 마디마다 뿜어내는 향기
믿는 대로 치유되는 기적에 매료되었다

I Am an Amaurotic Person

Although everything is born in the dark
Noble spirits strive not to fall into darkness again
Because it is evidence of being alive

Crossing the boundary between darkness and brightness
And knowing how to get wet in the rain and burn in the sun
"I" am a fine human being

Due to strong opposition of those who hate
My shout that darkness is the source of a greater energy
I learn how to survive as an amaurotic person
Who paints truth gray

In the black smoke rising from behind the darkness
To the cursed crowd trying to escape from the oxidizing flames
Miracles are invisible

After spitting on the ground to knead the clay and apply it to the eyes
You suggested me to go to the pond and wash
Every word of the language emits a scent
I was fascinated by the miracle of being healed as I believed.

나를 통해 일어난 기적들
육적인 상처의 회복
선택된 백성의 일원이 되는 영적 거듭남에
긴가민가한 의문을 가지는,
나는 눈뜬 소경

어둠 속
별과 같이 반짝이는 믿음으로 당신을 따라 나선다

Miracles that happened through me
Recovery of physical wounds
At the spiritual rebirth of becoming a member of the chosen people
Having a question of whether it is true or not,
I am an amaurotic person

In the dark
I follow you with faith shining like a star

갈대의 노래

푸른 하늘 머금은 강가의 갈대숲에는
방주 같은 작은 상자 하나 떠내려 온다

역청과 나뭇진으로 강물을 막고
그 속에 기도로 강보를 만들어
뉜 아기
하얗게 물든 갈대 머리로
강물처럼 흔들리며 흘러온 80년
갈대숲 비밀을 빗질하고 있다

노을이 떠난 자리
찾아온 찬 바람에
피부를 맞대고 서걱이는 애달픈 사랑

불타지 않는 가시나무 앞에서 신발을 벗고
주인이 이끄시는 대로 살아가는 삶
선택된 민족의 횃불이 된다

검은 장막 내리는 밤이 오면
두 손을 꼭 잡고
갈대숲 지나 별빛 쏟아지는 꿈길을 걷는 이들이 있다

Song of the Reed

In the reed forest at the riverside that bears the blue sky
A small box, which is like an ark, floats down

After blocking the river water with bitumen and resin
A baby's quilt was made in the box
And a baby was laid
With reed hair dyed white
Lived for 80 years while being shaken like river water
They are combing the secret of the reed forest

In place where the sunset left
At the cold wind that came
Painful love that crunches in skin-to-skin contact

After taking off the shoes in front of a thorn bush that never burns
The life lived as led by the owner
Becomes a torch for the chosen people

When the night in which the black curtain falls has come
Grasping both hands tightly
Some people walk on a dream path where starlight pours past the reed forest.

별과 나

어두운 밤하늘
정원에 나가 팔을 벌려
쏟아지는 별들을 안았습니다.

안기지 못한 별들은 차츰차츰
빛을 잃어갔습니다

화려한 욕심이 점점 사라져
슬픔으로 몸부림치는 별을 보고
가련한 생각이 들었습니다

그날 이후 봄이 와도
밤마다 별을 품지 않았습니다

다시 밤하늘에는 사자자리, 왕관자리, 목동자리 별들이
빛나기 시작했습니다.

세월 지나 지금에야
별들이 속삭이는 소리를
들을 수가 있었습니다

Star and Me

Dark night sky
I went out to the garden and open arms
To hug the pouring stars.

The stars that could not be hugged gradually
Lost their light

As splendid greed gradually disappeared
While seeing stars writhing with sadness
I felt pity

Although spring has come after that day
I did not hug stars every night

In the night sky, the stars of Leo, Crown, and Shepherd again
Began to shine.

Only now after time passed
I could hear
The sound of the stars whispering

돌아서는 길

달빛 내리는 깊은 산속
흐르는 강물이 은파를 연주하고
지나가는 바람은 세레나데를 부른다

보고 싶은 마음
골짜기에 구름으로 내려
긴긴밤을 꿈으로 채운다

외로움을 별에다 걸어두고
꿈길에서 빠져나와
그리움을 토하는 두견새가 된다

밤이슬 맞으며
정처 없이 흐르는 달빛 따라
힘없는 날갯짓으로 숲을 떠난다

The Way to Turn Around

The heart of the mountain where moonlight falls
The flowing river water plays the silvery moonlit waves, and
The passing wind serenades

My longing for you
Comes down in the valley as clouds
To fill the long-long night with dreams

I hang my loneliness on the star
Get out of the dream road, and
Become a little cuckoo that vents longing

Exposed to night dew
Following the moonlight that flows aimlessly
I leave the woods with weak wingbeats

숨겨둔 열쇠

노획된 불로초들이 빈사 상태로
식탁 위에 널브러져
탐욕을 향해 자유를 아우성친다

수저로 포크로 먹을 것, 안 먹을 것
도덕도, 윤리도 먹어 치우는 시대
분간하는 능력이 상실됐다

결국, 먹어야 살겠지만
신神은 먹이 속에
노화로 향한 독성을 풀어 놓았다

산천山川을 삶고 바다를 끓여봐도
영원으로 이어줄 생명의 열쇠
어디에 감추어 두었는지 찾을 수 없다

Hidden Key

The captured elixir plants in a moribund state
Are scattered on the dining table
And shout for freedom toward greed

In the era in which even morality and ethics are eaten
The ability to distinguish between
Those that should be eaten using a spoon, those that should be eaten using a fork, and those that should not be eaten was lost

In the end, humans should eat to live, but
In the food, God
Put the toxicity towards aging

Even if they simmer mountains and rivers and boil the sea
The key to life that will lead to eternity
Cannot be found from where it was hidden

갈망의 시간

푸른 들판
아무도 봐주지 않은 청순한 풀꽃
저마다 꽃을 피우기 위해 모진 시련을 겪습니다

고통의 진액 속에서 형체를 드러내는 사랑
영혼의 갈증을 해소시킵니다

밤의 탐욕에 얽매인다면
봉급 날 하루를 위하여 사는 것일 뿐
얼마나 부질없고 헛된 삶이 아니겠습니까?

가진 것 없어도 성실과 겸손을 다하여
그리움으로 곱게 피운 제비꽃 한 그루
기도와 버무려 고요히 당신께 바칩니다

Time of Yearning

In a green field
Each of innocent grass flowers that no one has seen
Go through harrowing ordeals to bloom.

The love that reveals its shape in the essence of pain
Quenches the thirst of the soul

If you are bound by the greed of the night
You are just living for the one payday
How futile and useless would it be?

Though it has nothing, with all sincerity and humility,
The one violet plant that bloomed finely with longing
Is silently mixed with prayer and dedicated to You

역사의 숨소리

모일 곳을 찾지 못해 흐르는 물은 막을 수 없다

빠르게 흐르는 강물에도 소용돌이가 있어
물길을 헛돌게 한다
청렴
묵인
부패
역사에 근거를 두고 있는 반복되는 행위

흘러가는 세월의 줄기마다
필요한 용서와 화해의 마디
대나무는 마디를 가지고 있으나
속을 비워 굽어지지 않고 하늘로 뻗는다

어떤 머묾도 흐름에 밀려나기 마련이지만
남아있는 먹물이 채 마르기도 전
절개節槪와 정절貞節을 그려 넣는다
이때 수묵화水墨畵가 완성된다

붓이란 부드럽게 보이는 힘의 도구
먹물이 권력이 되면
무섭게 휘두르는 칼에 검은 피가 묻고
서정이 스며 있는 붓에는 시詩와 예술을 해산解産 한다

The Sound of Breathing of History

The water that flows because it cannot find a place to gather cannot be stopped

There are whirlpools even in fast flowing river water
To make the waterway run idle
Integrity
Connivance
Corruption
Recurring acts based on history

For every stream of the flowing time
A node of forgiveness and reconciliation is necessary
Although bamboo has nodes
The inside is emptied to stretch out toward the sky without bending

Although all stays are bound to be pushed away by flcws,
Before the remaining ink dries up
Fidelity and chastity are drawn in
Then, the ink wash painting is completed.

A brush is a tool of power thar looks soft
When ink has become power
The dreadfully wielded sword is stained with black blood
The brush permeated with lyricism gives birth to poetry and arts.

우주의 시간이 하루라면
지구는 4초밖에 되지 않은 촌각
흐름과 머묾의 사이에서
역사는 흐르는 물의 등을 타고
붓도 버리고 먹물도 비우며 블랙홀로 들어선다

If the time of the universe is a day
The time of the earth is an instant, which is only 4 seconds long
Between flow and stay
History rides on the back of flowing water, and
Enters the black hole throwing away the brush and emptying the India ink

에스겔 골짜기의 환상곡

생명이 사그라진 척박한 땅에
서원誓願을 저버린 죄로
내가 끌려온 질곡의 골짜기
현미경으로 세포 속의 비밀을 캐는데
바람은 검게 타버린 수많은 유골을 핥고
세월은 널브러져 있는 뼈에다 하얗게 시간을 덧칠하고 있었다
섬뜩한 마음으로 신神의 권능을 본다 차라리 꿈이었으면 좋겠다

골짜기에 나뒹구는 뼈
삶의 희망을 품을 만한 근거는 아무 데도 없다
어둠이 음산하게 깔려있고 바람은 고요를 갉아 먹고 있다

귓가에 들려오는 음성
나의 입을 통해 외쳐 댈 신神의 계시
뼈들아, 이어져라
힘줄아, 붙어라
근육아, 뼈 위에 오르고
가죽아, 덮어라. 생기가 들어가서
큰 군대가 돼라!

육체가 유독 불가역적 방향으로 흐르는 것은 영혼 때문이다

Fantasia in Ezegel Valley

In a barren land where life has dissipated
the Valley of Ordeals to where I was brought
Due to the sin of forsaking the vows
Secrets in the cells are ferreted out with a microscope
The wind licks numerous blackened remains
Years have been painting over the scattered bones white with time.
I see the power of God with a frightened heart, I wish it was rather a dream

Bones scattered in the valley
There is no basis for entertaining hope for life
The darkness is dingily crawling the wind is gnawing the silence.

A voice is heard at the rim of my ear
A revelation of God to be shouted through my mouth
Bones, be connected
Tendons, stick
Muscles, go on the bones
Leather, cover, after accepting vitality
Become a big army!

The body particularly flows in an irreversible direction because of the soul.

동영상을 거꾸로 돌리면 먼저 생기가 빠져나가고, 가죽이 벗겨지며, 살이 떨어져 나가고, 힘줄이 분리되어, 백골만 남게 되겠지
가역적이라면 알파와 오메가의 의미가 사라지지 않을까?

골짜기에 가득한 뇌성과 우레
고요히 흐르는 물소리
풀잎 끝에 매달려 영롱한 소리를 낼 것 같은 이슬 앞에서
나는 두 손을 높이 들고 창조의 환상곡을 지휘한다

If the video is played backwards, the vitality should go out first, the skin will peel off, the flesh will fall off, the tendons will be separated, and only the white bone will remain.
If the process is reversible, wouldn't the meaning of alpha and omega disappear?

With the peals of thunder and storm completely filling the valley, and
The sound of the quietly flowing water,
In front of the dew that seems to make a brilliant sound hanging from the end of a blade of grass
I raise my hands high and conduct the fantasia of creation

나비

많은 역경 겪은 후
탈피 때 찢긴 속 날개에 흔적이 사라지고
두 쌍의 날개가 생겼습니다
날고 싶은 욕망을 가슴 가득히 채웠습니다

꿈이 이슬처럼 사라지기 전
수천 년 이어온 화려한 날갯짓으로
하늘 높이 올랐습니다

협곡이 힘주어 짜내는 환성歡聲에
폭포가 굽이쳐 대지를 적시고
무지개가 뿜어내는 광채에 현혹되어
은밀해야 할 자연의 즐거움까지 맛보았습니다

꿈속에서 지나온 협곡을 샅샅이 살펴도
더는 분노를 찾을 수 없고
보이는 것은 신비에 찬 위대함 그 자체였습니다
하늘을 날기가 두려워졌습니다

날개의 비늘이 빛을 받는 각도에 따라
색깔이 달라지듯
저마다의 서러움과 눈물로 엉겨 붙은 갈등을 털어내고
현란한 색으로

Butterfly

After undergoing many adversities
Traces in the inner wings torn during molting disappeared
And two pairs of wings were formed
The heart was completely filled with the desire to fly

Before the dream disappears like dew
With the brilliant wing strokes that have been passed down for thousands of years
It flied up high in the sky

At the shout of joy worked out with hard effort by the canyon
The waterfall welters to wet the ground
Fascinated by the luster emitted by the rainbow
I even tasted the pleasures of nature that should be secret

Even if the canyon passed by in my dream was thoroughly probed
Anger could not be found anymore, and
Only the mysterious greatness per se was visible
I became afraid to fly in the sky

As the color changes
Depending on the angle at which the scales of the wings receive light
The conflicts entangled with each one's sadness and tears are shaken off
In brilliant colors

가볍고
경건하게
태양보다 더 밝은 곳으로 날아오릅니다

Lightly
Reverently
They fly to places brighter than the sun

신神의 혓바닥

이율배반에 비합리성과 합리성을 함께 가지신 분
사랑과 심판
축복과 진노
사망과 부활
신神의 진노로부터 구원받은 핏값이 너무 무겁다
과거와 현재 사이에 신神의 말씀이 있고
현재를 이끌고 있는
신神의 혓바닥 위로
미래가 미끄러져 가고 있다

신神은 시간을 원圓으로 만들어 놓고
인간과 자연을 돌게 한다
죽음의 매듭을 훑아가며
다가오는 미래와 연결하는 신神의 혓바닥
원圓 가운데 교회를 짓고
붉은 십자가를 종탑 위에 높이 세웠으나
예언자나 선지자의 음성은 들리지 않는다

Tongue of God

The one who has all of antinomy, irrationality, and rationality
Love and judgment
Blessing and wrath
Death and resurrection
The price of the blood for salvation from the wrath of God is too heavy
There are the words of God between the past and the present
On the tongue of God
Leading the present
The future is sliding

God made time into a circle, and
Let humans and nature rotate
Licking the knot of death
The tongue of God that connects to the coming future
Although a church was built on the center of the circle, and
A red cross was erected high on the bell tower,
The voice of the prophet or the visionary cannot be heard

이드id

무의식중에 유입되는 본능의 욕구들
아름다움과 사랑
향락과 번식으로
자존심조차 처참하게 헐리고 있다

시들어버린 풀잎이 나누어 가질 수 없는 아름다움을
한탄하는 소리
찢긴 사랑만
썩은 사닥다리 위를 오르며 두려움에 떤다

탐닉의 길 끝에서 허물어지는 향락은
이성적 판단마저
갉아먹으며
은밀해야 할 쾌락이 옷조차 벗어버렸다.

육신에 파고든 원초적 에너지로
시작과 끝이 맞닿는 본능의 원圓안에 서게 되어도
흔들리지 않는 순결에
하늘로부터 내가 꼭 듣고 싶은 한마디 말
'두려워 말라, 너는 내 것이라'

이드id : 정신 분석학 용어의 하나로, 개인의 무의식 속에 선천적으로 가지고 있는 본능적 에너지의 원천

Id

Due to the instinctive desires that unconsciously flow in
Beauty and love
Pleasure and reproduction
Even my pride is being horribly demolished.

The sound of lamenting over
The beauty that cannot be shared by withered blades of grass
Only torn love
Is trembling in fear while climbing up the rotten ladder

The pleasure that collapses at the end of the road of indulgence
Gnaws
Even rational judgment
Gnawing
And the pleasure that must be secret even took off its clothes.

With the primitive energy that burrowed into the body
Even if I become to stand in the circle of instinct where the beginning and the end meet
At the unshakable purity
The words I want to hear from the sky without fail
'Do not be afraid, you are mine'

Id: One of the terms of psychoanalysis, which means a source of instinctive energy that is inherent in the individual's unconsciousness.

값진 고백

단순히 가리기만 하면 되는 줄 알았다
시작부터 벗은 몸
왜 가리려 애쓰는지 알 수 없다

때때로
단순함을 복잡하게 만드는 고백
어떻게 생각하나

슬프지 않은 것을 슬픔으로
사랑과 비극을 동의어로 만들어야
사랑이 강조되는 것인지

진실을 토함은
긴 고뇌의 시간이 찰나刹那로 스치나
사랑과 믿음은 영원하다

A Valuable Confession

I thought I just had to hide it
The body which has been naked from the beginning
Why they try to hide, I do not know

Sometimes
Confession makes simplicity complicated
What do you think about it?

Only when what is not sad is made to be sad
And love and tragedy are made into synonyms
Is love emphasized?

When the truth has been vomited
A long time of agony passes by in an instant, but
Love and faith are eternal

손잡이

화려하게 보이는 집이 있다
널따란 정원에는 잔디가 깔려있고 금방 깎은 잔디에서 풋풋한 냄새가 퍼진다

그녀의 문 앞에서 세레나데를 부를 수도 없다
방 안으로 들어가고 싶은데 보이지 않는 손잡이
어찌할 수 없어 기다리는 마음만 초조할 뿐
신神이 만든 건축물이 너무 묘妙해서
머리를 굴려봐도 대책이 없다

어둠이 차츰 다가오는데 차라리 그녀가 뛰어나와 나를 쫓아내면 좋겠다
얼굴이라도 볼 수 있는 기회가 생기기 때문이다

어둠은 집안의 빛 더러 밖으로 새어 나와 나의 형체를 반사 시키는 법을 가르친다
예기치 않게 안에서 예쁜 손이 문을 연다
나도 모르게 얼굴이 붉어 오고 심장은 불규칙한 박동을 시작한다
순간적으로 일어난 일이다

금속 가루가 달라붙는 자석의 습성을 그녀도 가지고 있었다 매우 심한 열기가 전신을 감쌀 때 나침반은 방향을 잃었다

Handle

There is a house that looks gorgeous
The large garden is covered with grass, and the fresh smell spreads from the freshly cut grass.

I cannot serenade in front her door
I want to go inside the room, but I cannot see the handle
As I do not know what to do, only my waiting heart is nervous
The buildings created by God are so weird
There is no countermeasure even if I put my brain to work

The darkness is gradually approaching, and I rather want her to run out and drive me out.
Because at least an opportunity to see her face will arise

The darkness teaches the light in the house how to leak out and reflect my shape.
Unexpectedly, a pretty hand from inside opens the door
My face turns red without my knowledge, and my heart starts to beat irregularly.
It happened momentarily

She also had the nature of magnet to which metal powders stick. When very intense heat wrapped around my body, the compass lost its direction.

이제 손잡이 없이도 문이 열리고
가을에 화려한 노을빛이 정원을 지나 베란다까지 다다른다
점점 찾아오는 적막이 오히려 화려하다

Now the door opens even without any handle
Brilliant sunset light in autumn passes through the garden and reaches the veranda
The silence that gradually comes is rather gorgeous.

주가株價

내면에 들리는 탐욕의 노래에
전자 화폐가 전파를 타고 공중에 날아다닌다
주가가 춤을 춘다

은밀히 조성되는 불화가
물 위의 파문처럼 퍼져나가고
태양 빛은 일그러져 무가치해진다

화산처럼 솟아난 산의 정점은
상한가의 화염을 내 뿜고 절벽 아래 떨어져
파도에 뜯긴 살점이 보인다

현실의 파고를 넘지 못하는
파도를 긁어내고
바다를 구겨서 주머니에 넣었다

Stock Price

At the song of greed heard to the inner side
Electronic money flies in the air on radio waves.
Stock prices dance

Secretly created discords
Spread like ripples on the water
Sunlight is distorted to become worthless.

The peak of the mountain surged like a volcano
Spouts the flames of the upper limit price and falls down the cliff
To show the flesh torn in the waves.

Unable to go beyond the height of the waves of reality
The waves were raked out
And the sea was crumpled and put into the pocket

밭에 떨어진 씨앗

어릴 적
소풍 가면
선물이 적힌 종이를 숨겨놓고
보물찾기하던 인식에서
아직도 벗어나지 못하고 있다

밭은 고통스런 노동력을 먹고 살지만
땅의 끝자락에 밭을 일구어
보화를 숨겨놓은 주인은
값진 가치를 깨닫는 사람을 기다리고 있다
그 밭을 사고 싶지만
나에게는 소개할 공인중개사가 없다
있는 밑천 다 팔아서
남이 눈치채기 전
시간을 가로질러 직접 당신의 밭을 사야 하는데

지혜의 목도리를 목에 두르고
쾌락의 안경을 껴도
밭에서 진정한 보화를 찾지 못한다
길가나 돌밭,
가시떨기에 떨어지는 씨앗들의 신음이
아프게 영혼까지 스며든다

Seeds That Fell in the Field

From the cognition in childhood
To hide pieces of paper written with the names of gifts
And play treasure hunt
When we went on a picnic
I still cannot escape

Although the fields live on painful labor,
The owner who cultivated a field at the edge of the ground
And hided treasure
Is waiting for those who realize the precious value
I want to buy that field
But I don't have no licensed real estate agent to introduce me to him
Although I have to sell all the seed capital I have
And cross time to firsthand buy your field
Before others sense

Despite people wear the scarf of wisdom around their neck
And wear the glasses of pleasure
They cannot find true treasure in the field
The groans of the seeds that fall on roadsides, stone fields,
Or bunches of thorns
Painfully permeate into the soul

기름진 옥토에 묻힌 씨앗들
흙덩이 사이를 뚫고 나오는 생명은
보화의 형상을 드러낸다

고통에 갇힌 껍데기를 벗고
두 손을 뻗어
하늘을 우러러 자라고 있다

새로운 주인은
끊임없이 밭을 갈고 씨앗을 뿌린다

Those seeds that were buried in fertile soil
Make the lives come out through the masses of soil
And reveal the shape of treasure

They take off the shell where they were trapped in pain
Stretch out both hands
And grow up to the sky

The new owner is
Constantly plowing the field and sowing seeds

나이테

태양의 둘레를 돌며 살아가는 공전을 배운다

계절 따라 내딛는 보폭
가다 쉬다 반복되는 발자국
쉬운 삶이 아니다.

이정표를 향해가는 궤도에
동행하는 선線에겐 배려가 깊다
이탈하는 유성에는 발자국 없는 마침표뿐
죽음은 가벼운 먼지와 같다

어떤 경우에도 벗어날 수 없는
쓰디쓴 고난에도
장미꽃 향기와 더불어 동심원을 그려야 한다

공전과 자전의 순서로
궤도를 채워야 하는 인내와 사랑
이슬 맞으며 걷는 발걸음마다
밤하늘의 별들은 환희의 노래로 우리를 감싸 안는다

육신이 노쇠해가도
하늘의 섭리를 읽으며 자라는 나무처럼
가슴으로 하늘을 안고
삶의 계절을 따라 나이테를 그려본다
자연이 문을 닫을 때까지…….

Annual Ring

I learn the revolution which is living while revolving around the sun

Strides taken according to seasons
Footprints made while going and resting are repeated
The life is not easy.

On the track going towards the milestone
The accompanying lines are deeply considered
To the shooting stars that break away, only periods without footprints are available
Death is like light dust

Even at the bitter suffering
Which can never be escaped from in any case
Concentric circles must be drawn with the fragrance of roses

The patience and love necessary to fill the track
In the order of revolution and rotation
At every step walked in dew
The stars in the night sky embrace us with a song of joy

Like trees that grow while reading the providence of heaven
Even when the body gets old
Embracing the sky in my heart
I draw rings according to the seasons of life
Until nature shuts the door… … .

사라진 우물

검은 숲으로 덮인 높은 산山이 작은 시골 마을을 안고 있다
산에 나무하러 간 사람치고 바람나지 않는 남자가 없는
여자의 몸과 엮어진 산山의 전설
그 산山의 정기를 받은 우물을 퍼마신 입들
지금이라면 미투me too 물결에 익사했을 것이다

집집이 있을 법한 여인들의 한恨을
우물가에다 토해 놓는다
놀란 우물은 입만 쩍 벌리고 있다
절제 없는 언어로 풀어버린 스트레스에 기분이 홀가분하다

여인들은 물을 퍼서 게워낸 말을 씻고
입을 씻고
속이 시원할 때까지 계속하다 돌아간다
시간 따라나선 종종걸음
뒷모습이 없다

Missing Well

A high mountain covered with black forest embraces a small rural village.
The legend of the mountain woven with a woman's body
Thar there is no man who went to the mountain to gather firewood and did not have a secret love affair
The mouths of the well that received the spirit of the mountain
Should have drowned in the wave of 'Me too' if they lived now

The resentments of women that are likely to be harbored in every family
Are vomited at well sides
The surprised well is just opening its mouth widely.
The women are lighthearted after relieving stress with uncontrolled languages

The women scoop water to wash the vomited words
And their mouths
And continue the foregoing until they feel cool before they go back
The short and quick steps that followed time
Have no appearance from behind

시간은 발걸음이 너무 빠르다
들풀에는 꽃이 피고 지는 짧은 순간처럼
시골이 큰 도회지가 되어버린 지금
입 벌린 우물은 추억에서만 불려 나오고
동네 앞을 지나던 개천은 노쇠한 노인같이
물이 말라 존재마저 없어졌다.

역사歷史가 되지 못해 전설로 태어나
작은 시골 마을에 계속 머물고 싶은 우물
땅을 뒤지고 측량을 해도 찾을 길 없다

우물은 추억의 한정된 시간 밖으로 나와
어릴 적 잠시 머물던 시골을 찾는다

Time walks too fast
Like the short moment when flowers bloom on and fall from wild grass
Now when the countryside has become a big town
The well with the open mouth comes out only from memories
The stream that was passing by in front of the village has been dried like an old man
And even the existence disappeared.

Born as a legend because of the failure to become a history
The well that wants to keep staying in the small country village
Cannot be found even though the ground was searched and surveyed.

The well comes out of the limited time of memories
And visits the country village where it stayed for a while in its childhood

토끼의 정사

불법이 합법적인 날갯짓으로 위장하고
어둠과 어둠이 다투고 있다
서로 더는 버틸 힘이 없어
사랑과 증오가 함께 어둠에 추락하고
옷을 입을 틈도 없이
체면의 겉옷과 멍에의 넥타이를 든 채
입으로 새끼를 낳는 개구리처럼
어둠이 나를 토해 낸다

생존의 몸부림이 아닌 사랑을
이끼가 품은 축축한 물에 적셔
순간의 쾌락을 방사하는 빈 정원에는
오늘이 사그라들고 있다

토끼의 탈을 쓰고 채우는 욕정에
꿈을 휴지처럼 소각해 버리고
사랑과 비극은 동의어가 되어
바람에 굴러다니고 있다

낙엽과 함께 뒹구는 체면은
어둠을 은밀히 어루만지며
우리 곁을 떠나지 않고 있다

Rabbit' s Sex

Unlawfulness disguises itself as legitimate wingbeats, and
Darkness and darkness are fighting
Since both do not have the strength to hold out anymore
Love and hate fall into darkness together
Without even a chance to get dressed
Carrying the outer clothing of face and a tie of yoke
Like a frog that gives birth to young with its mouth
The darkness vomits me

In an empty garden where love, not struggle for survival
Is soaked in the water held by moss
To radiate momentary pleasure
Today is fading

Due to the lust satisfied in the rabbit's mask
Dreams are burnt like tissue paper, and
Love became a synonym of tragedy and
Is rolling in the wind

The face that rolls with fallen leaves
Touching the darkness secretly
Does not leaving our side

커지는 편차偏差

뾰족탑이 사라진 성스러운 큰 건물에
온갖 사연들을 안고 오는 사람들이 섞여 있다
슬픔, 가난, 업신여김을 받는 이들의 뜨거운 갈구
낡고 가난한 주머니에 뚫린 구멍을 기워도
찬바람만 자유롭게 드나들고
내놓기 쑥스러운 적은 연보捐補
꼬깃꼬깃 모아둔 정성이 부끄럽다
젖은 땀 냄새가 피 냄새로 변하는 막노동자의 비애를
한 가난한 과부의 동전 두 닢에 슬쩍 끼워 넣어
함수函數를 도입해 합리화하는 설교에 마음이 바쁘다

가진 자들
현관문을 열고 버튼만 누르면 문이 열리고
헤픈 여인처럼 누구든지 받아들이는 엘리베이터를
타고 오르내리는 욕망의 군상들
복종이 굴종을 거쳐 맹종에 익숙할 때까지
머리를 숙이는 무리만 명패를 내보이며 의자를 차지하고 있다

로봇이 의미심장한 웃음을 씩 지으며 지나간다

Increasing Deviation

In a large sacred building where the spire has disappeared
There is a mixture of people who came with various kinds of stories
Hot cravings of those who are in sorrow, poverty, or being despised
Although the hole built in my old poor pocket was patched up
Only the cold wind comes in and out freely
The annual report of the embarrassing enemy to put out
Small offering shameful to offer
The sincerity that made to collect it hardly is shameful
At the sermon that furtively inserts the sadness of a young laborer of whom the smell of wet sweat is changed into the smell of blood,
Between the two coins of a poor widow and rationalizes it by introducing functions
My mind is busy

Those who have
The groups of people of desire who go up and down
In elevators of which the door is opened only when the button is pressed after opening the front door,
Which accept anyone like an easy woman
Only those who drop their head until obedience is changed into submission, and then blind obedience becomes familiar
Occupy the seat showing their nameplate.

The robot passes by with a meaningful smile.

건물 앞뒤
주차장 시멘트 바닥에 고급 차들이 꿈틀댈 때마다
예의가 바르고
얼굴에는 화색이 돈다
어시장횟집에 호객행위는 칼끝에서 회膾가 튕겨 나오게 하고
파도 소리를 입으로 다시듯
출입문은 입을 쩍 벌리고 있다
밤새껏 불을 켰다 껐다
스위치는 피곤에 지치고
무참히도 가증스런 겸손에 짓밟힌 자존심은
알 수 없는 너절한 발자국의 흔적을 성형할 회개가
들어왔다 나갔다 하는 신음으로
빌딩 안을 꽉 채운다

가진 자와 갖지 못한 자 사이에
수평선이 그어지고
지평선 위에는 어둠이 내려
작은 반딧불처럼 깜박이는 정겨움이
큰 빌딩 숲과 점점 멀어져 사라지고 있다

In front and rear of the building
Every time luxury cars wriggle on the cement floor of the parking lots
They are polite
And have a good complexion on the face
The act of soliciting of a sashimi restaurant at the fish market
sashimi causes the sashimi to bounce off the tip of the knife.
As if smacking the sound of waves with the mouth
The door is opening its mouth widely.
Turning the light on and off all night
The switch is tired
The pride mercilessly trampled on by despicable humility
Fills the building completely
With the groan made while coming in and going out of the building by the
Repentance that will shape the traces of unknown sloppy footprints

Between those who have and those who do not
A horizon is drawn
The darkness falls on the horizon
The affection that flickers like a small firefly
Is getting farther away from the big building forest to disappear.

제2장 사랑의 미혹迷惑

Chapter II
The Delusion of Love

사모思慕의 노래

오랜 시간 지났어도
당신의 다정한 눈길과 부드러운 음성
잊을 수가 없습니다

당신을 그리워하는 것은
나의 눈물이 아직 다 마르지 않았기 때문입니다

지난날 조금씩 당신과 버성겨 걸어온 길
서러운 그리움으로
다시 발걸음을 돌릴 수가 없습니다

누구의 시선도 닿지 않는 얼굴에
당신의 그윽한 눈길이
내 가슴에 안개비로 내린다면
육체의 욕망을 불러일으켜
깊은 상처를 아물게 할 것입니다

텅 빈 마음에 말라버린 눈물
흘러가는 구름 한 조각이라도
머물면 좋겠습니다

Song of Longing

Although a long time has passed
Your affectionate eyes and soft voice
Cannot be forgotten

The reason why I miss you
Is that my tears have not yet been dried

To the path I walked through while being estranged from you
little by little on days gone by
Due to sad longing
I cannot turn my heels

On the face that no one's eyes reach
If your sweet eyes
Fall in my heart as misty rain
It will arouse the desire of the body
To heal deep wounds

In my empty heart where tears dried up
If even a piece of the flowing clouds stays
I would be pleased

사랑의 미혹迷惑

나는 모르는 것에 충실했다
사랑이란 단어에 복잡한 의미를 부여한 사람들
수학처럼 계산하는 그릇된 셈법
화산처럼 솟아오르는 욕정에 불결한 해석이 난무하는 사고에
익숙해져 가고 있다

낚인 복어가 부풀어 크게 보이도록 하는 몸같이
허영의 부레를 사용해 풍선을 흉내 내지 않았는지

나는 물고기를 이해하는데 눈뜬장님이 된다
기쁨도 슬픔도 녹아내는 세월이
내부의 모든 형질을 끄집어내어
균형이라는 저울로 나를 인어人魚로 만들었다
사랑과 위선이라는 두 개의 머리를 가진 변종 말일세
사랑의 단어에 대한 인지능력이 상실되어 서로 닮아갔다

눈도 귀도 콧구멍도 두 개인 것은
듣고 보고 생각 하라는 것이다
단순하지만 무서운 것이 입이기에
먹고 마시고 뱉어내는 감당하기 어려운 것은 한 개만 주었다
나는 두 개의 머리가 필요하다
정립된 사랑의 원초적 의미를 담을
장식품으로라도 한 개 더 달고 싶다

Delusion of Love

I was faithful to what I did not know
Those who gave the word love a complex meaning
Become familiar to
Wrong way to calculate love, which is like mathematics, and
The thought in which unclean interpretations of lusts that soar like a volcano are rampant

Like the body of that blowfish that swells when caught to look bigger
Didn't they use the air bladder of vanity to mimic the balloon?

I understand fish, but I become an amaurotic person
The time that melts both joy and sadness
Pulled out all the traits inside
To make them into mermen with the scale termed balance
The variant with two heads, termed love, and hypocrisy.
The ability to recognize words of love has been lost so that they resembled each other.

The reason why there are two eyes, ears, and nostrils
Is to enable just to listen, see and then think.
Since simple but scary is the mouth
Only one that eats, drink, and spits out, was given as it is uncontrollable
I need two heads
I want to have one more head even as an ornament
That will contain the original meaning of established love

가식의 거울을 꺼내어 보면
한 개의 머리는 썩고 있었다
신에게 바칠 흠 없는 완전한 제물로서 자격조차 없다

거룩한 영역에서 방출되어버린 인간의 헛된 사랑이다
홀로 컴퓨터 앞에서 시詩를 작업하며 웃고 우는 시인은
외로울 시간이 없다

When I took out and see the mirror of pretense
I found one head was rotting
It is not even qualified as a perfect, flawless offering to God.

It is vain love of human vain love removed from the holy realm.
A poet who laughs and cries while working on poetry alone in front of a computer
Has no time to be lonely

굴착掘鑿

산이 길을 막고 있다. 늘 보았던 익숙한 산이다.
돌아가자니 거리가 멀고 오르자니 넝쿨이 얽혀있어 숲을 헤쳐나갈 수 없다
뚫어야 한다.
터널을 관통하기 위해
물을 뿜어 열을 식히며 굴진하는 굴착기가
기계식 굴착공법에 속하는 물건이란다

사람인지 늑대인지 모르지만
이 산에 왔다 간 발자국이 많이 흩어져 있다
사랑하려면 사랑하지 않는 것이 사랑이라는 말 남기면서
지나가는 멍청이도 있었다
우습지 않나? 뜻도 모를 말 같아서

수가 성 여인이 물길으러 갔다가 메시아를 만난 사실을 물동이마저 던져버리고 증언하며 다녔다는 이야기를 나도 읽었다

Excavation

The mountain is blocking the road. It is a familiar mountain that I have always seen.
To go around, the distance is far and to climb, I cannot go through the forest because vines are entangled, therefore, the mountain should be penetrated
To excavate tunnels
The excavator that excavates while cooling the heated body by spouting water
Is said to be a thing that belongs to the mechanical excavation method

Although unknown whether humans or wolves,
Many footprints of those who have been to this mountain are scattered around
Leaving a phrase that to love, you should not love, and that is love
There was an idiot that passed by
Isn't it funny? It seems like a phrase of which the meaning cannot be understood

I also read the story that the woman named Suo threw her water jar and wandered to testify that she met the Messiah when she went to draw water.

그 후 내 생의 책갈피 속에서 튀어나온 당신을 만난 거다
거친 바위를 뚫고 소통의 터널을 만들었지만
언제 흙이 무너져 터널이 막힐까 염려 속에 살면서도 행복했었다
불안이 현실을 뒤덮고 있을 때
터널 속 전구의 필라멘트가 끊어지고 밖으로 쫓겨난 발자국은 춥고 슬펐다

빈 터널 속에는 계절 따라 바람이 드나들고 낡은 흔적들이 사라져가면
어둡고 습한 곰팡이들이 자생하는 다른 생태계가 이루어질 테지

Thereafter, I met you who popped out of the bookmarks of my life.
Although I made a tunnel of communication by penetrating through rough rocks
I was worried that the soil would collapse, and the tunnel would be blocked while living but I was happy.
When anxiety covered reality
The filament of the light bulb in the tunnel was broken and the footprints of expulsion to the outside were cold and sad.

As the wind comes in and out of the empty tunnel according to the seasons and the old traces disappear
Another ecosystem where dark and moist fungi grow wild will be formed

복수초의 꿈

서러움이 지나간 자리에 버릴 수 없는 그리움
가슴에 담고
아무도 모르게 앓아온 열병熱病
꽃대에 올려 고뇌의 환희를 예언한다

하얀 눈이 어둠을 물리고
한 줄기에 한 송이만 피우는 꽃
하늘을 향해 환상의 눈을 맞추며
노오란 사랑의 정체성을
내 영혼에 색인索引한다

옛길 벗어나 새로운 길이
고난의 길이든, 광야의 길이든
벽을 향해 돌아누워 어찌할 바 모르는
늙은 디아스포라

하얀 눈이 덮인 길에 노란 꽃으로
낮이면 열고, 밤이면 닫아가며
향기 은은한 동산에서 그대 품에 안길 때까지
아름다운 꿈을 꾸고 있다

Dream of an Adonis

Keeping the longing that cannot be thrown away in the place passed by sadness
In the heart
It puts the fever it suffered from unnoticed by anybody
On the flower stalk to predict the joy of agony

When white snow repelled the darkness
Only one flower blooms per stalk
Contacting the eyes of fantasy with the sky,
The flower indexes the identity of yellow love
On my soul

A new road appears beyond the old road
Whether the road of suffering or the road of the wilderness
Turned to the wall not knowing what to do
The old diaspora

With yellow flowers on the road covered by white snow
While opening during the day and closing at night
Until the time to be embraced in your bosom in the hill with a delicate scent
Is having a beautiful dream

살아있는 물방울

빛이 녹아있는 물방울은 우주를 닮고
생명의 섭리를 감추고 있는 신비가 있다

둥근 물방울은 하나님의 나라
당신이 소유한 사랑의 프리즘에서
굴절되어 나오는 빛이 황홀하다

일곱 빛깔의 둥근 무지개
당신의 상징이요
영광이어라

풀잎 끝에 맺힌 가냘픈 이슬에도
굴절되어 나오는 은혜가 있어
영롱한 환희가 보이는구나!

어둠 속에 묻혀 있는 별들도
아침을 기다리는 그믐달도
제 몫을 다하려 빛을 내는데

나의 자존심이 굴절 당할 때는
분노가 되고 한恨이 되어 나오다니
이거야말로 과연 슬픈 일이 아닌가

Living Water Drops

Water drops in which light is melted resemble the universe
And has the mystery that hides the providence of life

Round water drops are the kingdom of God
Coming out from the prism of love, you have
The refracted light is fascinating

Round rainbow of seven colors
Is your symbol and
Glory

Even in the feeble dew formed on the tip of a blade of grass
Since there is grace that comes out refracted
Brilliant joy is visible!

Even the stars buried in the dark
And the old crescent waiting for the morning
Emit light to fulfill their duties

When my pride is bent
It comes out as anger and resentment
Isn't it really sad?

항상 날 위해
기도하던 어머니의 눈언저리에
마르지 않던 눈물방울에서
굴절되어 나오는 인자함을 보았고
영원한 나라를 보았음이라

From the tear drops that were not dried out
At the eye rims of mother who was praying
Always for me
I saw the benevolence that comes out refracted
And the eternal kingdom

조용한 아침

아침이슬 영롱할 때
초가집 굴뚝에 연기가 오른다

깔깔대는 아기 웃음은
문틈으로 새어 나고
참새들이 재잘대면
구수한 된장국 냄새가 풍기는 뜨락에
지금은 사라져 보이질 않지만
느긋한 삶이 있고
평화가 흐르는 시골이 그립다

Quiet Morning

When the morning dew was bright
Smoke rose from the chimneys of thatch-roofed houses

The cheerful laughter of babies
Leaked through the chinks in the doors
When the sparrows were chattering
In the garden where savory soybean paste soup smelled
There was a relaxed life
Although not visible now because it disappeared
And peace flowed in the countryside, which I miss

종소리

십자가 하나 꽂혀있는 나무 첨탑에는 심장이 숨어있었다
아래로 길게 연결된 줄을 잡고 침묵을 흔들어 놓는 손길이 원망스러웠지만
꿈길에서 불러내는 소리가 맑고 동그랗게 퍼져나가는 음의 파동
종소리는 물수제비 뜨면 생기는 둥근 물결조차 보듬는
깊은 호수가 된다

새벽기도는 붉게 물들어 통회痛悔의 눈물로 젖고
굽이굽이 돌아온 모퉁이 길에
기다리던 아픔은
동이 틀 때쯤 녹아내려 속이 후련해진다

가족을 떠나 독일에서 공부하던 때
마을마다 성당의 첨탑에서 은은히 들려오는 종소리에 그리움의 등燈이 켜지고
새벽마다 울리던 어머니의 숨결 같은 옛 종소리가
어느새
별빛 내리는 내 마음 호수에 은물결을 일으키고 있었다

Bell Sound

In the wooden spire with a cross stuck on it was hidden a heart
Although the hand that shakes the silence by holding the rope lengthily connected to the ground was resentful
The sound that called me out from the streets of dreams was the sound waves that were clear and spread round
The bell sound becomes a deep lake
That embraces even the round waves that are formed when people skip stones

Dawn prayers turn red and get wet with the tears of contrition
On the corner road came winding around
The pain of waiting
Melts at the break of day making me feel relieved

When I left my family and studied in Germany
The lamp of longing was lit at the bell sound dimly heard from the spire of the cathedral in every village
The old bell sound that was ringing every dawn like the breathing of my mother
Before I know
Was generating silvery waves in my heart lake where starlight falls

고향의 하늘 아래
사람들의 검은 이기심 다 모아놓고 소음의 누명을 씌워 배려와 애정을 쫒아내던 날, 심금을 울리던 종소리는 소음으로 묶여 감동의 장막帳幕 뒤로 사라져 버렸다
이기적인 씨앗이 자라 울타리를 치고
인정人情이 자라는 옥토는 점점 메말라갔다

이웃 간에는 벽이 높게 쌓이고
층간 소음도
피아노 소리도
아기의 울음조차 듣는 청각은 더욱 예민해 갔다

오랜 세월 지나도
무지개 너머 구름 한 조각에
하늘 소망이라도 걸어두고
마음에 감동을 주던 은은한 종소리가 그리워진다

Under the sky of my hometown
On the day when all people's black selfish minds were gathered to expel consideration and affection under the false charge of noises, the bell sound that had been touching people's hearts was grouped into noises and disappeared behind the curtain of emotional movements.
Selfish seeds grew to make fences, and
The fertile soil where benevolence grows gradually became barren

Walls were built up high among neighbors
The auditory sense to hear noises between floors
Or piano sound
And even babies' crying became more or more sensitive.

Although many years has passed
On a piece of cloud beyond the rainbow
I hung a hope in the sky
I miss the soft bell sound that was touching my heart

광야의 테라코타

광야의 메마른 땅에는 갈증이 도사리고 있었습니다
발걸음마다 짊어진 지게가 무거워
부모의 그늘에서 쉴 수 없었습니다

태양 볕에 박 넝쿨은 시들어가
잎들은 줄기에서 떨어져 살아야겠다는 생각 외에
존재감이란 화려한 사치였습니다

재화財貨가 우상이 되던 날
고통으로 나이테가 만들어지고
창백한 달빛만이 상처 난 꽃잎을 어루만질 뿐
시선視線을 대주재大主宰를 향해 꽃피울 줄 몰랐습니다

견디기 어려운 불길에 허물어지는 토기土器 되어
자신自身의 체면이나 자존심 밖에 보이지 않고
전갈이 우글대는 뜨거운 사막을 헤쳐나올 수 없어
무너져 내리는 영혼을 깨닫지 못했습니다

당신을 알고부터 초점을 땅에서 하늘로 두던 날
허리에 신비의 띠를 두르고
밤하늘의 별을 안았던 그때부터
꽃에는 경이로움이 일어났습니다

Terracotta in the Wilderness

In the dry land of the wilderness, thirst was lurking.
Since the A-frame carried on the shoulder was heavy every step
I could not rest in the shade of my parents

As the gourd vines were withering under the sunlight
And leaves fell from the stem, except for the thought that I should live
Presence was an extravagant luxury

On the day when goods became idols
A growth ring was made with pain
Only the pale moonlight soothed the injured petals
I did not know that the line of sight would bloom toward the great dominate

Because I became an earthenware that collapses in unbearable flames
Only my face or pride was visible, and
I could not get through the hot desert infested with scorpions
Thus, I did not realize my collapsing heart

사막에서 구름 기둥으로 뜨거움을 피할 수 있었고
어둡고 추운 밤, 불기둥으로 보호를 받을 수 있었습니다
아침이면 빵 대신 만나*로 허기를 면하기도 하였습니다

광야에서 희미한 반딧불이처럼 내 영혼이 깜박일지라도
보이지 않는 이로부터 내리는 은총으로
미완성 테라코타는 순결한 빛을 내고 있습니다

만나*(manna)-이스라엘 민족이 모세의 인도로 이집트를 빠져나와 가나안으로 갈 때 광야 생활을 하는 동안 여호와로부터 받은 특별한 식량

On the day I knew you and shifted my focus from the earth to the sky
From the time when I wore a band of mystery around my waist
And held the stars in the night sky in my bosom
Wonder occurred to the flower

I could avoid the heat in the desert with a pillar of clouds, and
Could be protected in dark and cold night with a pillar of fire.
In the morning, I sometimes satisfied my hunger with manna* instead of bread

Even if my soul flickers in the wilderness like a dim firefly light
With grace granted by the invisible
The unfinished terracotta emits pure light

〚Manna*: manna-special food the Israelites received from Jehovah while they were living in wilderness while they were going to Canaan under Moses' guidance after escaping from Egypt.

이별의 서곡序曲

만나는 것은 나의 기쁨입니다
고통으로 출발한 사랑이지만
한도 끝도 없는 아름다운 꽃을 피웠습니다

말없이도 통하고
글을 쓰지 않아도 알 수 있는 마음
차가운 손을 녹일 수 있는 입김은 더욱 뜨거웠습니다

지금,
낙엽 지는 벤치에 앉아
차가운 정적靜寂에 가려
보이지 않는 그대 미소
낡은 병풍 속 그림처럼 감동이 퇴색되어갑니다

사랑하지 않는 것이 아닙니다만
같은 하늘 아래서 헤어져 사는 것이 고통이기에
나도 모르게 터져 나오는 신음
이별은 그리움을 낳기 때문입니다

시간이 기력을 쇠衰하게 하고
빛나던 눈의 광채가 나를 떠날 때
사랑의 일식 현상이 시작됩니다

Prelude of Farewell

Meeting is my pleasure
Although love started with pain
Infinitely many beautiful flowers bloomed

We understood each other without any word
Each other's heart could be known even without writing
The breath that could warm cold hands was hotter.

Now,
Sitting on a bench where leaves fall
Covered by the cold silence
Your smile is invisible
Like a picture in an old folding screen, the impression fades

Although it is not that I do not love
Because living apart under the same sky is a pain
Groans burst out in spite of myself
Because parting gives birth to longing

Time makes vigor decline, and
When the sparkle of the eye that were shining leaves me
The phenomenon of solar eclipse of love begins

사랑의 입자粒子

사랑이란 단어에 현혹되어
삶에 균형을 잃고
방탕의 신을 신고 밤이슬 맞으며 헤매는 발걸음
환상의 꽃을 쫓아 가본들
잠시 머물다 사그라질 인생이 아닌가?

육체 바깥에서 당신을 기다리고 있는
신神의 사랑을 보지 못한 채
굶주린 돼지와 함께 욕망을 채우려
쥐엄나무 열매를 먹던 탕자가 아니던가?

가을 노을빛에 시달린 붉은 홍시같이
허공에 매달린 시린 마음
당신의 향기로 연민憐憫의 밤을 추스르고 있다

만삭이 된 바다가 해를 해산하고
붉은 피를 덮어쓴 파도가 붉게 물드는 아침에
'힉스 장*'과 닮은
원초적인 사랑으로
당신과 나는 신神의 입자粒子가 된다.

Particles of Love

Fascinated by the word love
Lost balance in life
The wandering steps in the shoes of debauchery exposed to night dew
Even if they chase the flower of fantasy
Aren't they lives that will disappear after staying for a while?

Without seeing the love of God
Waiting for you outside the body
To satisfy your desires with a hungry pig
Didn't you eat the honey locust fruit like a prodigal?

Like a red ripe persimmon suffered from the autumn glow of the setting sun
A chilling heart hanging in the air
Is taking care of the night of compassion with your scent.

In the morning when the full-term sea gives birth to the sun
And the waves covered with red blood turn red
With the primitive love
That resembles "Higgs Field*"
You and I become the particles of God.

신神을 경외하는 이에게는
죽음이 두려운 것이 아니라 영원을 추구하는 것
우리는 시공간의 중심에 서서
무無에서 유有를 창조하는
사랑의 입자가 된다

* '힉스 장'(또는 '힉스 입자')은 다른 기본입자에게 질량을 부여하는 역할을 하기 때문에, 이런 역할로 말미암아 무에서 유를 창조하는 신의 입자라고 불린다.

For those who adore God
Death is not fearful but pursuing eternity
We stand at the center of time and space
Become the particles of love
That create existence from naught

* "Higgs field" (or "Higgs particle") is called the particle of God that creates existence from naught because it plays the role of giving mass to other basic particles

유혹의 과일

갈비뼈가 생기를 얻었다

요염한 자태에 미혹되어
강렬한 근육질이 풀린 사내
향기 짙은 사과를 쉽게 삼킨다

둘 다 수치심을 보는 눈이 열렸다
상습적으로 마르는 나뭇잎보다
체면을 날염捺染한 가죽옷을 얻었다

벗은 몸을 수치스럽게 느끼는 것은
해산과 노동의 고통을 의미하는 피의 징계다

이때부터 패션이 눈을 떴다
유명 브랜드가 수없이 끼어들고
유행의 부레에는 허영으로 가득 찼다

더러워진 옷을 때때로 벗어야 살 수 있는
저주의 화신
스올*로 가는 길섶에서 똬리를 틀고 있다

언젠가 에덴의 동산에서 쫓겨나야 할
처절한 운명
죽어야 사는 삶을 위해
중독된 사과를 끊임없이 먹고 있다

* 스올(Sheol): 죽음, 무덤, 지옥을 의미함.

Fruit of Temptation

Ribs gained vitality

Deluded by the voluptuous figure
The man whose strong muscularity was loosened
Easily swallows a strongly fragrant apple

The eyes of both to see shame were opened
Instead of habitually drying leaves
They obtained leather clothes printed with face

Feeling ashamed of a naked body
Is bloody disciplinary action, meaning the pain of childbirth and labor.

From that time, fashion was awakened.
Countless famous brands intervened
And the air bladder of fashion was filled with vanity.

The incarnation of curses
That can live only by taking off clothes that became dirty from time to time.
Is coiled up in the edge of the road to go Sheol*

The terrible fate
To be expelled from the Garden of Eden some day
For the life that can be lived only by dying
They constantly eat poisoned apples

* Sheol: means death, grave, and hell.

공허空虛한 석별惜別

숲속 오솔길 옆
오래된 작은 옹달샘
비바람에 허물어져 옛 모습 아니지만
가끔 새들이 와서 마시는 물만은 맑다

샘 위에 떨어진 가랑잎 하나
물결 따라 맴돌다 바람에 끌려 밖으로 쫓겨난다
자신의 의도가 아니다

폰으로 넘나드는 문자와 영상은 샘물처럼 솟아나지만
신뢰가 소멸하면
사랑은 허황된 꿈이 뱉어내는 재[灰]가 되고
영혼은 혼수상태에 빠지는 버릇을 가지게 된다

세상은 변하는 질서다
문명이란 글자에는 새로운 것만 우세할 뿐
또다시 퇴색되고, 허물어지고, 말라가는 옹달샘이 된다

햇빛 바래지는 저녁노을에
묵묵히 걸어가는 나그네
상처 난 마음을 달빛에 태운다

Hollow Regretful Parting

By the forest trail
A small old spring
Although not in its old shape because it collapsed due to rains and winds
The water drunken by birds that sometimes come is clear.

A withered leaf that fell on the spring
Hovers around along the waves until it is dragged and expelled by the wind
Not in its intention

Although the texts and videos that come and go through the phone spring up like spring water
When trust has become extinct
Love becomes ashes spit out by vain dreams
The soul becomes to have a habit of falling into a coma

The world is a changing order
Only new ones are dominant in the letter civilization, and
The spring again discolors, collapses, and dries.

Under the evening glow where the sunlight fades
A traveler walking silently
Burns hid broken heart in the moonlight

숲속에 잎들은 지고 햇볕이 옹달샘에 닿으면
물이 증발되고, 허물어진 꿈에서
사랑은 불가역의 수레를 타고 길을 떠난다

When the leaves in the forest fell and the sunlight hits the spring,
The water evaporates and from the collapsed dream,
Love sets off on a journey on an irreversible wagon

환희를 알고부터

오, 이렇게 쾌락의 순간을 느낄 줄 알았다면
일찍 선악과의 두려움에 얽매이지 않았을 텐데
당신이 만든 형상이라면 두려움도 고통도 없는
완전한 생명체로 태어났어야 하지 않았을까?

호기심을 뿌리치지 못해 지키지 못한 명령 하나에
내가 지닌 모든 것을 잃고
오직
황폐한 토양에서 가시덤불에 찔려가며 살아야 하는 노동과
'짝'이라는 굴레를 씌워놓고 고통의 계곡을 만들어
아픔 속에 숨겨둔 환희의 찰나를 계곡에서 찾게 하지 않았던가?

아무도 열지 못했던 환희의 상자를 열어준 당신
당신에게 바쳐야 할 몸이라면
긴 세월 동안 방황의 언덕에서
어찌 슬픔과 외로움으로 헤매게 놔두었단 말인가?

이골 난 짜릿한 쾌감보다 순결이 내 안에 있을 때
당신의 백성이 되어
함께 즐거워하며 노래 부르는 것이 나의 전부이기에
사랑의 강이 흐르는 초지草地에는 푸른 싹들이 돋아나고 있다

After Knowing Joy

Oh, if I knew I would feel the moment of pleasure as such
I should not have been bound by the fear of the fruit of the tree of knowledge of good and of evil eartlier
If the figures had been made by you, should not they have been born as perfect lives
Without any fear or pain?

Because I failed to observe one order as I could not resist my curiosity,
I lost everything I had
The only
Way I can live is working on desolate soil while being stabbed by thorn
And you put a bridle called 'pair' on me and made a valley of pain
To make me find the moment of joy hidden in pain in the valley.

You opened a box of joy that no one could open
If I had to dedicate my body to you
Why you left me to wander with sadness and loneliness
On the hill of wandering for long years?

When chastity is in me rather than the accustomed thrilling pleasure
Becoming Your people
And singing songs while being delighted together is all I can do
Therefore, green sprouts are sprouting in the grassland where the river of love flows.

아비의 신음

나의 정원에는 꽃과 잡초가 섞여 살고 있습니다
잘 가꾼 꽃은 정원에 뿌리를 내리고
손끝이 닿지 않은 꽃은
스스로 울타리를 넘어 잡초가 되어
황폐한 땅으로 길을 떠납니다

자유가 좋아서 마음대로 산다 한들
이해할 수 없고
아들의 아이들이 잡초의 유전을 받을까 두렵습니다

아들이 잡초가 되는 것이 싫기 때문에
벌써 해가 서산에 기울어 어둠이 스며오지만
침침한 눈으로 기다림에 떨고 있습니다

정원에서 싹이 돋아나 자랄 동안
침범해오는 병을 내쫓던 고난의 기간이
오히려 행복한 날이었는지 모릅니다

이해를 하든 하지 않든
늙은 아비보다 항상 젊은 아들이 더 위대합니다
가랑잎은 바람에 정처 없이 흩날리지만
호미들이 얼기설기 놓여있는
정원에서 자라는 나무는 햇빛을 통해
더욱더 강건해집니다

Father's Groan

In my garden live flowers and weeds in mixture
Well-grown flowers take roots in the garden
Flowers not touched
Break away from the fence by themselves to become weeds
And set off a journey to a desolate land

Although they say that they live as they like because they like freedom
I cannot understand, and
I am afraid my son's children will inherit weeds.

Because I hate my son's becoming weed
Although the sun has already declined to the western mountain and darkness percolates
I am trembling in waiting with my blear eyes

The period of hardship expelling the invading diseases
While they put forth buds and grow in the garden
Might have been rather happy days

Whether understood or not
Young sons are always greater than the old father.
Although withered leaves are blown by the wind aimlessly
The trees growing in the garden
Where hoes are laid here and there
Become healthier through sunlight

껄떡쇠

가시로 길을 막고 담을 쌓아도
여기저기 기웃대는
마음속에 숨어 있는 탐욕의 껄떡쇠

평생을 같이하는 기러기보다
여섯 중 다섯이 혼외 자식을 가지는
원앙새가 결혼식에 나타나다니
시간이 흐르면
파헤쳐질 숲속의 둥지

신神의 선택된 백성이 가는 곳마다
금송아지 아피스
풍요의 신 바알 같은 잡신을 섬기던 우상숭배가
껄떡쇠 행동과 무엇이 다를까?

시간을 잠시 멈추고
괴로운 예언자, 호세아를 읽을 때
헤엄치던 원앙새가 사라진다

Drooling person

Even if the road is blocked with thorns and walls are built
Snooping around
The drooling person with greed hidden in my heart

Rather than wild geese that live with their spouse for life
Mandarin ducks that have illegitimate children at a probability of five out of six
Appeared at the wedding
As time passes
The nest in the forest will be dug up

Wherever the chosen people of God go
Is the idolatry that served spirits like Apis the Golden Calf, and Baal the god of abundance
Any different from the behavior of drooling persons?

When time was paused for a while, and
Hosea, a painful prophet is read
The mandarin duck that was swimming disappears.

눈을 뜨다

당신은 우수憂愁에 사랑을 버무려
나의 눈을 뜨게 했습니다

슬픈 듯 정갈한 당신
다른 이들은 모르지만
호기심은 괴로움에 손짓하기도 하고
가끔, 후회까지 불러들이지만
나에게는 현기증이 나도록 좋았습니다

평탄한 길만 걷는 우둔한 짓은 없을 것입니다
항상 곧은 길은 없기 때문입니다
언젠가는 굽어지기도 하고 갈라지기도 합니다

안이함은 때때로 나태와 향락을 부릅니다
쾌락으로부터 얻어진 자유
도취경陶醉境에 빠져 허우적거리고
비탄은 증오와 분노의 가발을 쓰게 합니다

땅과 바다보다 더 넓은 공간을 차지하는
당신과 나
허공에서 사랑을 불러낼 수 있다면
이것이 신神이 내린 선물이 아니겠습니까?

나는 영혼의 눈마저 닫을 수는 없습니다

Opened the Eyes

You mixed love with melancholy
To open my eyes

You are sad-looking but are neat and proper
Although others do not know
Curiosity sometimes beckons suffering
And even summons regrets some other times
I liked you to the extent that I was dizzy

There will be no stupid thing to walk only on flat roads.
Because there is no road, which is always straight
Any road is bent or diverged someday.

Comfort sometimes beckons indolence and enjoyment
Freedom obtained from pleasure
Makes the person fall in ecstasy and struggle
Grief makes the person wear the wig of hatred and anger

Occupying a space larger than land and sea
You and I
If we could beckon love from the air
Wouldn't it be a gift from God?

I cannot close even the eyes of soul

여운餘韻

애절한 눈으로 머뭇거리기만 하는
용기 없는 내 마음
아무도 모르게 흐르는 잔잔한 강물과 같습니다

변명에는 가난하고
인내와 겸손 속에서 풍요로운 진실로
당신의 귓가를 어루만질 때
어찌 사랑하지 않을 수가 있겠습니까?

사랑이 꽃잎처럼 활짝 피어나 쉬이 지는 것이라면
오히려 욕망의 고통에서
오래도록 그리움만 가지고 싶습니다
용기 없고 어리석게 보여
비웃음을 산다 해도
그리움은 나의 유일한 재산이기 때문입니다

영원으로 바뀌는 그 시간까지는
그리움의 옷만은 벗을 수가 없습니다
나만의 샘터에서 홀로 목을 축일 수 있다면
그것만으로도 행복할 따름입니다

lingering Imagery

Just hesitating with sad eyes
My heart which is craven
Is like a calm river water that flows unnoticed by anybody.

Poor in excuses
When I touch your ears
With abundance of truth in patience and humility
How can you do not love me?

If love blooms like flower petals and fades easily
Rather in pain of desire
I want to have only longing for a long time
Although I look stupid and craven
And incur ridicule
Because longing is my only property

Until that time when it turns into eternity
I cannot take off the clothes of longing
If I could quench my thirst at alone at my own fountain
I will only be happy only with it

3월이면

잃어버린 젖 내음
어디 있을까

소쩍새 울음 울며
멀리 가신 어머니

희미한 기억 속에
살아나는 얼굴

늙어가는 자식의
애달픈 그리움

In Every March

Lost smell of milk
Where is it

Crying like a cuckoo
Mother who want far away

In the faint memories
Her face revives

Sorrowful longing
Of an aging child

아름다운 여인

품에 안기듯 아늑한 마을
산이 병풍처럼 둘러있고
하얀 구름은 은밀하게 아래로 내리고 있다

잎이 무성하지 않은 나뭇가지를
스쳐 가는 바람 소리처럼
여인이 읊조리는 간절한 기도 소리에 울음이 섞였다

야생의 돌배처럼 아프게 익어오던 지난날
언제나 가슴에 흘러드는
한탄과 슬픔이 눈물 되어 볼을 적신다

괴로움과 고통의 조각들을 조심스럽게 모아
아픔과 눈물로 헝클어진 마음까지
사랑의 휘장에 싸서 신神께 바치는 정성
어찌 축복받지 않을 수 있을까?

수만 번의 깊은 고통과 시련을 겪은 후
한 알의 보석이 신비한 빛을 내듯
삶의 빛을 아름답게 발發하고 있다

Beautiful Woman

A cozy village as if I am embraced
Is surrounded by mountain like a folding screen, and
White clouds are secretly falling down

Like the sound of winds
Passing through branches not thick with leaves
Weeping is mixed with the sound of earnest prayer recited by a woman

During the past days of ripening painfully like wild pears
Always flowing into in my heart
The lament and sadness became tears to wet my cheeks

After gathering the pieces of suffering and pain carefully
Even the heart that is messed with pain and tears
The devotion to pack them in a veil of love and dedication to God
How can it not be blessed?

Like a single jewel emits a mysterious glow
After experiencing tens of thousands of times of deep pains and trials
The light of life is emitted beautifully.

비애悲哀 속의 그리움

오늘 아침까지 일어났던 일들이 희미하게 사라지고
부르고 싶은 이름조차 멀어지는 기억은
입술 밖으로 나오지 못해 혀에서만 맴돌다가
쌓아 올린 그리움이 하나씩 허물어지고 있다

수탉이 세 번이나 아침을 알릴 때까지
목자의 시야에서 벗어난 양의 처절한 부정의 틈바구니에서
마지막 닭 울음에 살아난 기억

마냥 시간이 그 자리에 서 있을 줄 알았지만
모래성 같은 미래가 이렇게 쉽게 올 줄은 몰랐다
시간이 두 개의 팔로
내 주위에 웃고 울던 얼굴들을 지워나가고
시간 사이로 빠져나간 웃음들은 소멸 되어 들을 수 없다

미래마저 상실될 소용돌이 속에서 건져내야 할 사랑에
그리움을 달지 않았다면 헛된 일이 될
비탄의 아픔일 뿐이다

선악과에 맺힌 비탄의 열매를 먹고
그 속에 숨겨둔 씨앗이 그리움인 줄 알았다면
후일, 그나마 손에 피를 묻히게 되지는 않았을 것을…….

Longing in Sorrow

The memory in which things that had happened until this morning fade away
And even the name I want to call disappears
Lingers only on the tongue because it cannot come out of the lips
So that accumulated longings are crumble one by one.

Until the rooster announced the morning as many as three times
In between the desperate denials of sheep that went out of the sight of the shepherd
The memory was revived at the last cock crow

Although I thought time would keep standing there
I did not know that the future like a sandcastle would come so easily
With two arms, time
Erased faces that laughed and cried around me
The laughter that got out through the gaps between time is extinguished and cannot be heard

If the love that should be rescued from the vortex where even the future will be lost
Is not attached with longing, it would be just
The pain of grief that will become futile

After eating the fruits of the grief borne in the fruit of good and evil
If they knew that the seeds hidden in it were longing
Later, they would not have to stain the hands with blood.......

산山 그림자

산이 해변에 뛰어들어 수영을 한다
입영立泳 같은데 너무 진보적이다
멀리 못 달리게 해가 산의 다리를 잡고 있다

해가 물속에 잠겨 손이 풀리면
산을 덮고 있는 나무들이 불안에 떤다
잎들은 물속에서 숨이 끊기고
바다는 몸서리치는 밤의 침식에
사라진 산의 암석과 부딪쳐 멍이든다

먼지와 뭍을 떠날 수 없는 인간들
가증한 논리로
신神의 계율을 어겨가며 동물의 가죽을 덮어쓰고
가장 동물적인 향연을 베푼다
창조나 진화의 바퀴를 거꾸로 돌리면서
성스러운 질서는 감추고 타락한 노래를 헤프게 부른다

쓰디쓴 고난이 오는 것도 모르면서
밤은 점점 깊어간다

다시 아침이 되어 해가 뜨자
산은 젖은 몸으로 바다에서 나와 피곤한 몸을 말린다

Mountain Shadow

The mountain jumps on the beach and swims
The swimming seems like standing swimming but is too progressive.
The sun is holding the mountain's leg to prevent the mountain from running too far

When the sun has been submerged under water and the grip is released
The trees covering the mountain tremble with anxiety.
The leaves expire in the water
Due to the horrifying erosion at night, the sea
Collides with the rocks of the disappeared mountain and gets a bruise.

Humans who cannot leave dust and land
With a contemptible logic
Cover themselves with the skins of animals violating the divine precepts,
And hold the most animal feasts
While turning the wheel of creation or evolution backwards
They conceal the sacred order and sing corrupt songs prodigally.

Without knowing that bitter suffering is coming
The night gradually gets deeper

When the morning has come again, and the sun has risen
Mountains come out of the sea with a wet body and dry the tired body.

봄의 왈츠

봄바람이
살며시 내려앉는다
덩달아 안개비도 흙을 적신다
푸르게 돋아나는 연약한 들풀은
추위에 떨던 논두렁에 옷을 입힌다

봄이 짙어질수록
아름다움이 정겨운 네 눈동자에 가득해지고
내가 부르는 노래에
싱그러운 봄의 왈츠가 시작된다

Waltz of Spring

Spring breeze
Comes down and sits gently
The misty rain also wets the soil.
The soft wild grass that grows green
Dresses the field that has been shivering with cold

As the spring deepens
Beauty fills your warm pupils, and
At the song I sing
The refreshing spring waltz begins

시린 망설임

밤이 깊고 갈 길이 멀어
갈까 말까 망설여도
가지 않으면 안 되는 길
광풍에 밀려가는 안개처럼 걸어간다

지붕 위에 밤을 새운 외로운 참새
차가워진 날개에 머리를 박고
지나온 옛일을 회상해 봐도
기쁨보다 슬픔이 더 많다

몇 번이고 쓰러져도
일어나는 법을 터득하는 아기처럼
육체의 달콤한 욕망에서 일어나야 한다

가야 할 남은 길 얼마 남지 않아도
너무 특이하거나
너무 아름다운 것은 부담스럽다

즐거움과 기쁨이 덜해도
평범하면서도 그리움이 생길 수 있는 것이라면
시린 망설임이라도 좋다

Cold Hesitation

Even if I hesitate to go or not
Because the night is deep and the way to go is long
The road I cannot but go
I walk like a mist driven by a mad wind

A lonely sparrow that stayed up all night on the roof
Puts its head on the cold wings
And recalls things of the past,
There were more sorrows than joys

Like a baby who learns how to get up
No matter how many times he falls
I must get up from the sweet desires of my body

Even if there is not much way to go
Things that are too unique, or
Too beautiful are burdensome

Even if less pleasure and joy are provided
If that is ordinary but can cause longing
Even cold hesitation is fine

백송이 장미

신神이 물 위에 운행할 때
태초 이전부터 선택되어 태어난
당신은
도저히 소박해질 수 없는
화려하고 붉은 장미꽃봉오리

나의 사랑의 진액 속에서
'따봉'을 외치며 활짝 피어난 꽃

꽃잎마다 새겨 둔 순결은
아름다운 100송이 장미꽃이 되어
생명책의 봉인을 떼기 전
흠 없는 꽃다발을 바치고 있다

사랑할수록 멀리서 음미해야 할
후각의 세포를 깨우는
저 아름다운 향기
행복의 과일에 스며들어 과즙을 충만케 한다

Hundred Roses

When the deity runs on the water
Selected and born before the beginning of the world
You are
Fancy and red rose buds
That can never become simple

In the essence of my love
The flower burst into bloom shouting 'Thumbs up'

The purity hidden in every petal
Became beautiful 100 roses
And offers a flawless bouquet
Before breaking the seal of the book of life

The beautiful scent
That awakens the olfactory cells
Which should be enjoyed at a father place if loved more
Permeates the fruit of happiness and to make it full of fruit juice.

빛의 꼬리에 시간을 매달고
수억 년을 달려와 꽃잎에 내린 신神의 은총恩寵
활짝 피는 송이마다 뿜어내는 황홀한 신음이
환희의 멜로디가 되어
은은히 하프의 현絃을 춤추게 한다

조용히 불타오르는 당신의 노래가
내 혈관에 녹아들어
영원의 세계로 흐르고 있다

Hanging time on the tail of the light
Hundreds of millions of years ran the grace of God to fall on the petals
The ecstatic groans gushed by every blooming cluster
Become a melody of joy
To make the harp's string dance subtly

Your song that burns quietly
Melts in my blood vessels
To flow into the world of eternity

샘터가 되어

지난날 가시덩굴에 휘감겨
숨 막히도록 아픈 꿈길에서 깨어나
검은 숲속을 헤매며
갈길 몰라 방황할 때
아침햇살같이 다가온 당신

오늘의 슬픔을 내일의 기쁨으로 가두어 놓을 수 있다면
나는 당신의 가슴속에
누구의 손도 닿지 않는 샘터가 될 것입니다
목을 축일 수 있는 사람은 오직 한 사람이면 만족합니다

찰랑대는 샘물을 듬뿍 길어낼 당신
샘 가에 피어나는 꽃잎으로 나의 눈물을 닦아주며
따뜻한 숨결로 내 가슴을 채워줍니다

삶의 고통 한 조각이라도 조심스레 거두어
인내와 진실의 옥토에서 사랑의 뿌리를 내려
넘쳐흐르는 청순한 샘물로 목을 축이게 되기를 원합니다

Become a Fountain

In the past, wrapped in thorns in the past
I woke up from a breathtakingly painful dream
Was wandered in the black forest, and
Straying about because I did not know where to go
When you came to me like the morning sun

If I could lock up sadness of today with joy of tomorrow
I will become a fountain in your heart
That cannot be reached by anyone
If only one person can quench thirst, that will be enough.

You who will draw plenty of spring water
Wiping away my tears with the petals blooming near the spring
You fill my heart with warm breaths

I wish you to carefully reap even a piece of pain of life
Take roots of love in the soil of patience and truth
And quench thirst with the innocent spring water that overflows

가연佳緣

가슴 깊이 묻어둔 한마디 말
어렵게 꺼내어
부끄러운 얼굴로 겨우 전한 후
어찌나 행복한지 하늘 향해 소리쳤다

그녀가 기뻐하는 모습에
덩달아 기뻐지는 내 마음
날고 싶은 기분에 포옹을 한다

그녀 앞에 설 때마다 하고픈 고운 말을
꽃잎에서 따오고, 별빛으로 엮어
귓가에 속삭이고 싶다

매일매일 만나서 주고 싶은 내 마음
저~ 먼바다에 펼쳐진 수평선 위를
남김없이 다 덮도록 감싸고 싶다

Good Match

A word buried deep in my heart
After taking out hard
And barely conveying it with a shameful face
I was so happy that I shouted to the sky

As she looks happy
I also become happy
I hug as I feel as if I can fly

The refined languages I want to say every time I stand in front of her,
I would like to pick from petals, weave with starlight
And whisper in her ears

With my heart I want give you every day when I meet you
I would like to completely cover
The horizon that spreads far out in the sea

궤도 이탈

마른 땅 위로 나온 곁 뿌리들
낯선 길로 들어선다

깊은 골짜기 어귀에서 기다리는 흰개미
떨어져 나온 곁뿌리를 쪼아 댄다. 곁뿌리는 꿈틀대며 구멍이 난다
헐벗은 산에서 울리는 낯익은 신음이 길다.
속내를 삭이다 타버린 모정母情
애처로운 마음을 밖으로 토하는 어머니

곁에서 슬며시 훈수하면
격하게 화를 내는 모정母情
블랙홀이라도 마셔버릴 듯하다

불순종의 패배가 창문을 통하여 넘어 들어와도
어미 혼자만 욕할 수 있는 특권인 듯하다.
예측하기 어렵다

여름은 바람 타고 정신없이 지나가고
늘 보던 시각이 마비되어도
세월에 바래진
불쌍한 어미의 흩날리는 머리카락만 보인다.

Deviation from the Track

Lateral roots that came out on dry ground
Enter a strange road

Termites waiting at the mouth of the deep valley
Peck off the lateral root that came off. The lateral roots wriggle while being perforated
The familiar groan sounding in the bare mountain is long.
Maternal love that has been burned while soothing the heart
Mother expresses a pathetic heart outward

When somebody gently gives advice at the side
The maternal love fiercely gets angry
Seems to swallow even a black hole

Even if the defeat of disobedience comes through the window
Only the mother seems to have the privilege to curse
Difficult to predict

Summer frantically passed by riding on the wind and
Even though the vision that had been always seeing was paralyzed
Faded over time
The hair of the poor mother is still visible.

궤도를 이탈하여 얽혀버린 나무뿌리
끈적이는 늪에서 소모하는 정열
돌이킬 수 없는 피폐한 갈증이 육체를 갉아 먹는다
어미는 몽땅 빗자루가 닳아 버릴 때까지 청소하고 싶었을 게다

Tree roots that deviated from the track and became entangled
Passion consumed in the sticky swamp
The irreversible exhausted thirst gnaws the body
The mother should have wanted to clean it until the stubby broom was worn out.

제3장 이 애처로운 손을 보시고

Chapter III
After Seeing This Pathetic Hand

이 애처로운 손을 보시고

주여,
당신의 손에 든 낫을 거두어 주십시오
아직 추수할 열매가 익지 않았습니다

옛 이집트의 열 번째 재앙처럼
코로나바이러스로
이 도시의 시민들은 참담하게 목숨을 잃어가고 있습니다
이들에게는 문설주에 바를 양羊의 피도, 회개悔改의 눈물도 없습니다

우주복 같은 방호복을 입고
안간힘을 다하여 바쁘게 움직이는 의료인들
자신의 생명을 내어놓고 환자를 돌보는
가련한 손들만 사투를 벌이고 있을 뿐입니다

당신의 잔에 가득한 분노를 거두시기를 원합니다
부모와 형제자매의 마지막 주검의 얼굴조차 보지 못하고 있습니다

이제 당신의 결심만 남았습니다
우리가 간절히 외치는 소리를 들으시고
열매가 여물어 추수기가 꽉 찰 때 낫을 들기 원합니다

After Seeing This Pathetic Hand

Lord,
Please lay down the sickle in Your hand
The fruits for harvest are not yet ripe.

Like the tenth plague of old Egypt
Due to coronavirus
The citizens of this city are terribly losing their lives.
They do not have the blood of sheep to be applied to the doorpost or the tears of repentance

Wearing protective suits like space suits
Medical professionals who move busily falling over themselves
Taking care of the patient at the risk of their lives
Only the poor hands are fighting desperately.

I want You to put away Your anger completely filling your cup
I cannot even see the last faces of the carcasses of my parents and siblings.

Now only Your determination remains
Please hear us crying earnestly
I want to pick up a sickle when the right harvest time has come as fruits are ripe.

현장의 영웅들

여행국에 도착하자마자 기다리고 있는 설움
족쇄로 채운 14일간의 강제 격리
코로나바이러스 발생 국가의 얼굴은 철면피다

보이지 않는 올가미로 죄어드는 목숨
영혼은 육신의 옷을 벗고 도망가려 하지만
피곤에 지친 의료인들의 피나는 헌신은
영웅들로 태어나고
악독한 우한 코로나바이러스에 대한 의병도 곳곳에서 일어났다
.
심금을 울리는 미담이 물밀 듯 밀려들며
종교의 엄숙한 예배 방식도 바꾸어 놓았다
고귀한 분노가
검은 망토를 걸친 저승사자를 짓밟고
흉악한 목구멍에서 뱉어내는 재앙을
피와 눈물로 태우고 있다

아스클레피오스의 지팡이를 보면 도망갈
코로나바이러스
귀신이 돼지 떼에 들어가 호수로 떨어져 죽는
기적이 일어나고 있다

Field Heroes

The waiting sadness that begins at the moment of arrival at the travel destination country
Forced quarantine for 14 days that shackles the subjects
The faces countries where coronavirus occurred are brazen faces

Life is squeezed by an invisible snare
Although the soul tries to take off the clothes of the body and run away
The desperate devotion of tired healthcare workers
Gave birth to heroes
and righteous armies against the vicious Wuhan coronavirus were raised here and there

Beautiful touching stories were deluged, and
The solemn way of worship of religions was changed.
Noble anger
Is trampling the grim reaper in a black cloak, and
Burning the calamity spit out of his nasty throat
With blood and tears

Coronavirus
That will run away when the Rod of Asclepius is seen
A miracle is happening
In which ghosts enter the herd of pigs and fall into the lake to die.

방역 마스크,
민초民草들이 원하는 작은 소망이 아름답다
모자라는 병상을 사랑으로 메워가고
죽음을 살려내는 희생의 손길들
재앙을 불사르고 활기찬 시간으로 돌려놓는다

시간의 바다에서 반사되는
헌신하는 의료인들은 영웅이 되고
지워지지 않는 하늘의 빛깔이 됨이라

Quarantine mask,
The small wish of the people is beautiful.
The insufficient sickbeds are supplied with love
Sacrificial touches that save death
Burn disaster and recover the lively time

Reflected in the sea of time
Dedicating healthcare workers become heroes
And the indelible color of the sky

어떻게 해

눈물 어린 사연
가슴에 묻고
하루하루 살아가는 얼룩진 가슴에
그리움만 쌓이고
보고픈 당신 생각
깊어지는데
이를 어쩌나!
꿈길에서 만날까 기대했건만
잠 못 들어 애달프게 뒤척이는 밤
사랑한다 말 못 하고 깨어난 꿈
눈물을 닦아도 슬픔만 흐른다

What Shall I Do?

A tearful story
Was buried in the heart
In the stained heart with which I live day by day
Only longing is accumulated
Thought about you whom I miss
Becomes deeper
What shall I do!
Although I was hoping to meet you on the dream road
At the night I could not sleep but tossed and turned
I woke up from the dream before I could say that I love you
Even if I wipe away my tears, only sadness flows

치매

과거의 조각들을 모조리 모아
무한한 시간을 품은 공간에서
거침없는 희열을 느끼고 살아온 생애

눈 속 차가움이 풀리기 전
절망의 끝에 서서
외로움과 그리움을 버무리며
기다리는 나
님이 오실 길목에서 노란 복수초꽃으로 피어나련다

현재에는 검은 열기로 타버린 흔적만 남아있고
잊혀가는 추억 속
유년 시절만 기억에서 맴돈다

수많은 코로나바이러스가 우글거리고
지구의 자전을 역방향으로 돌리는 처참한 무도회를
그치게 할 로고스의 중력이 내 손에 있다면
기쁜 마음으로 태초의 행위로 돌이킬 수 있으련만

Dementia

After gathering all the pieces of the past
In a space that embraces infinite time
The life lived while feeling unhindered joy

Before the coldness in the eyes disappears
Standing at the end of despair, and
Combining loneliness and longing
I am waiting
On the road you will come through, I will bloom as yellow Adonis flowers.

Currently, only traces of burning with black heat remain
In the memories that are being forgotten
Only childhood lingers

If the gravity of the logos to stop
The terrible ball where numerous coronaviruses are rampant
And the Earth's rotation is reversed is in my hand
I should be able to turn the acts of now into the acts at the beginning of the world with joy

먼 옛일이 희미하게 살아나는 회상 속에
가슴에 심어준 첫사랑의 꽃 한 송이
이름조차 잊으며 품고 있어도
시간은 꽃잎을 하나씩 하나씩 떨구고 있다

애처롭게 과거를 잊은 사람 되어
글자마저 쓸어버린 빈 일기장에
채워 넣을 문장조차 찾지 못한 채
기억 끝에 서성이며 긴 한숨을 짓는다

In the recollection to vaguely revive things in the distant past
A flower of first love that you planted in my heart
Although I am harboring it even while forgetting the name
Time is dropping the petals one by one

After pitifully becoming a person who has forgotten the past
Unable to find even the sentences to fill
The empty diary from which even letters were wiped out
Draws a long sigh while strolling at the end of memory

극복의 계단

코로나바이러스들이 엄습하는 두려움은
보이는 것보다 보이지 않는 세계가
더 무한하기 때문이다

보이는 것은 잠깐이요
보이지 않는 것은 영원한 것
한 번만이라도 가시면류관을
가슴에 품는다면
무서운 병이라도 이겨낼 수 있을 것을

우리를 사로잡는 비애가
고난과 번민의 짐을 짊어질 고통이라면
죗값일까?
행복의 문을 열기 위한 열쇠일까?

한 송이 꽃을 피우기 위해
봉오리에도 시련이 있고
열매가 성숙하기까지는 아픔이 있는 것

우리도
낯설지 않은 고통스런 계단을 밟고 오를 때
높은 기쁨에 도달하지 않을까

Stairs of Overcoming

The fear of surprise attacks of coronavirus
Arises because the invisible world is
More infinite than the visible world

Visible things are momentary
While invisible things are eternal
If the crown of thorns is embraced
In the bosom even only once
Even the terrible disease can be overcome

If the sorrow that captures us
Is the pain to carry the burden of suffering and anguish
Should it be the price for sin?
Or the key to open the door to happiness?

To make a single flower bloom
The bud undergoes trials
There is pain until the fruit matures

We too
When stepping on the painful stairs which are not unfamiliar
Probably reach high joy

펜대믹*pandemic

붉은 서쪽 하늘에 검은 장막이 내리던
그날 밤
마지막 인사도 나눌 겨를도 없이 울어야 했다
울음은 온 지구를 삼켰다

우한 코로나바이러스일까
탄저균이 원인이었을까

장자들의 죽음
동물도 예외일 수 없었다
예부터
우는 자는 대부분 어머니
자식 때문에 모두가 울어야 했다
서로 위로할 자가 없다

재앙을 피해야 할 자들
피를 문지방에 발라야 하는 뜻은 무엇일까
먼 후일 피의 예언을 말함인가

전날엔 울음이 있어도
내일 아침이면 기쁨이 오겠지만
아무도 가르쳐 주지 않았다

Pandemic

That night
When the black curtain fell on the red western sky
People had to cry with no time to say hello
Crying swallowed the whole earth

Was Wuhan Coronavirus
Or Bacillus anthracis the cause?

The death of the firstborn son
Animals were no exception
From old days
Most crying mothers
Had to cry because of their children
No one could comfort each other

Why those who should avoid disaster
Should apply blood to the threshold
Does it refer to the prophecy of blood in the far future?

Even if there was a cry on the day before
Joy would come in the morning of the next day
No one told that

역사의 모퉁이에 몇 자 남길 사건
전염병보다도
회한과 후회에 대한 울음의 펜대믹이다

* 펜대믹(pandemic) 1.전국적인 유행병, 2.전 지역에 걸쳐 일어나는 유행병

An incident that will leave a few words at the corner of history
Is not the pandemic of the infectious disease
But is the pandemic of crying due to remorse and regret.

* Pandemic 1. A national epidemic, 2. An epidemic that occurs throughout the region

마스크를 쓰는 봄

겨울 동안 끊임없는 차가운 바람에 찢긴 봄
대지는 아랑곳없이 싹도 내고 꽃을 피우며
무심하게 다가오고 있다
막을 자가 없다

작은 괴로움이라도 남에게 전가하여
자신이 십자가를 질 생각조차 못 하는
어리석은 사람들
입만 살아 퍼트리는 바이러스는 더 가혹하다

뚫린 입을 막아야 한다
보이지 않는 병균이나 바이러스보다 더 무서운
자신의 정체성까지 훼손하는 언어의 남발
막아야 한다

내 입이 거칠어질 때
막아주던 부드러운 손
아직도
아름다운 손이
내 마음에 소묘素描로 남아있다

Spring Wearing a Mask

Spring torn by the constant cold winds during winter
The earth gives to attention to it and sprouts and produces flowers
While approaching nonchalantly
No one can stop

Passing even a little bitterness onto others
While not thinking of carrying the cross
Foolish people
Viruses that spread only by mouth are more severe.

The open mouths should be shut up
More terrifying than invisible germs or viruses
The overuse of languages that damages even one's identity
Must be prevented

The soft hands that blocked
When my mouth was becoming rough
The hands still
Beautiful
Remain in my mind as a sketch.

부활의 동산에서 풀 뜯는 양羊들이
듣고 살아온 방울 소리에
말없이 본능적으로 반응하고
신神의 무언의 계시를 보이던 봄은
마스크를 썼다

Sheep grazing in the Garden of Resurrection
At the sound of the bells they have been hearing while they live
React instinctively without words
The spring that showed the unspoken revelation of God
Wore a mask

애달픈 사연

사랑하는 아내와 아이들
마지막 얼굴 보며 작별하라고
바이러스와 혈장 치료로 줄다리기에
안간힘을 다하는 의사들

모든 정성 다해도
지병을 앓던 남편은
몹쓸 코로나바이러스에
처, 자식을 두고 먼 길 떠났다

콜센터에서 일하며 살아야 하는
고달픈 아내
모든 것 다 내려놓고
남편과 함께 떠나고 싶었지만
눈에 밟히는 자식들 때문에
얼마나 천지가 깜깜했을까?

많은 사람이 소리 없는 눈물로
따뜻한 위로와
격려를 보내고 있다

A Heartbreaking Story

To enable him to say goodbye
To his loving wife and children while seeing their last faces
In the tug of war with virus using plasma treatment
Doctors were doing their best

Despite all the sincerity
The husband, who had a chronic illness,
Due to the bad coronavirus
Set off on a long journey leaving his wife and children behind

Having to work at a call center for living
The exhausted wife
Although wanted to put everything down
And leave together with her husband
Haunted by the images of her children
How dark did she feel the heaven and earth?

With silent tears, many people are sending
Warm comfort
And encouragement

나의 기도

슬픈 마음으로 남모르게 울고 있습니다
당신도 함께 슬퍼하고 있겠지요
병들어 죽어가는 내 이웃과 내 민족
광야에서 불 뱀을 놋뱀으로 만들어
장대 위에 매달고
쳐다보기만 해도 살아나는
그 기적의 힘을 우리에게도 주시기를 원합니다
만나를 받아먹으며
굶주림과 뜨거운 시련 속에서
광야의 불 뱀이나
독을 가진 전갈처럼
나의 길에는 무서운 교만이 득실거렸습니다

고운 모양
우아한 풍채도 갖지 못한
마른 땅에서 자란 울퉁불퉁한 뿌리 같은 인생이었기에
당신의 찔림은 참지 못한 나의 혀 때문이며
십자가에서 상함은 나를 대신한 것임을 알고 있습니다

My Prayer

I cry secretly with a sad heart
You should be sad too
My neighbors and my people who got diseased and are dying
Would recover only by looking at
The fire serpent made into a brass serpent in the wilderness
Hanging on the pole
Please give us such a miracle power too
While receiving and eating manna
In hunger and hot trials
Like the fire serpent in the wilderness
Or a scorpion with poison
My path was filled with terrifying arrogance

Having no fine shape
Or elegant look
Since my life was like a bumpy root that grew on a dry ground
I know that you were stabbed because of my impatient tongue
And You were hurt on the cross on behalf of me

이 세상 살 동안
아픔을 신앙으로 치유케 하고
영육이 깨어져도 겸손으로 참게 한 당신
들판에 무수한 풀들이 솟아나고
힘없는 고목에서도 아름다운 꽃을 피우게 하지 않았습니까?
내 민족의 기치로 우한 코로나바이러스19를 물리쳐
새 삶으로 평안을 누릴 수 있게
허락해 주시기를 기도합니다

While living in this world
You made me heal pain with faith
And endure the breaking of my spirit and body with modesty
You made countless grasses spring up in the field
And made beautiful flowers bloom even in weak old trees
Please enable the banner of my people to defeat Wuhan Coronavirus19
So that we can enjoy peace with new lives
I pray for Your permission

질투심

아양 떠는 말이 다른 곳으로 쉽게 이동해 갔다
지나치게 미워져
떡 한 조각이라도 줄 마음조차 없어졌다

싫증은 언제까지 새로움을 찾아다닐는지
여물지 않는 여름이나
단풍으로 물들인 가을에도
계절이 쩔쩔매고 있다

아양 떠는 입가에
주름살을 안고 찾아온 차가운 바람
채색된 가을옷을 벗기고 지나간다

"나 외에 다른 신神을 섬기지 말라"는 말
독선적일까, 배신감에서 나온 걸까
나의 뇌 속에 해마가 의식을 지구 밖으로 끌어내는 날 알게 되겠지

Jealousy

Fawning words easily moved to another place.
I became to hate you too much
That even the mind to give you a piece of rice cake disappeared.

How long will the boredom search for novelty?
Even in summer when fruits do not ripen or
In autumn colored with autumn leaves
The seasons are be flustered

At the sides of the fawning mouth
Embracing wrinkles, cold winds came and
Pass by after taking off the colored autumn clothes

Are the words, "Do not serve any god other than me"
self-righteous or a product of a sense of betrayal
I should know it on the day when the hippocampus in my brain
pulls consciousness out of the earth

피곤한 변명

코와 입 위에 얹혀있는
마스크가 피곤하다.
죄 없는 귀도 따라서 피곤하다
바이러스는 말을 아끼게 하지만
숙주를 침공하는 작전에는
군대를 파견하기에 바쁘다
종일
서로가 피곤타고 변명뿐
사람들은 죽었다 살았다 갈피를 잡을 수 없다

왔다 갔다 하는 나침반에
미칠 지경이다

Excuse of Tiredness

Placed on the nose and mouth
The mask is tired.
The innocent ears are also tired
Although the viruses make people spare their breath,
In the operation of invading the host,
They are busy dispatching troops
All day
People only make an excuse that they are tired
But are unable to make out heads or tails whether alive or dead.

Due to the compass that moves back and forth
They are nearly demented

석양을 걷는 나그네

그리움도
단풍도
친구도 내려놓고
왜 홀로 가야 하는지 알 수 없지만
빛을 타고 다니는 그림자 되어
석양에 내려앉는다

사랑까지 걸머지고 가기에는
벅찬 인생
외로운 별빛 따라
아쉬운 마음으로 가야 하는 슬픈 나그네

A Traveler Walking Through the Sunset

Although I do not know why I have to lay down
Longing
Maple leaves
And friend and go alone
I become a shadow that rides on the light
And settle in the sunset

To carry even love
Too burdensome a life
Following the lonely starlight
A sad traveler who has to go with a regretful heart

눈물 어린 라면 국물

라면 스프 우려낸 국물에
라면 하나 끓여 먹는 아침 식사

남아있는 국물에
우동 사리 하나를 끓여 먹는 점심
냉장고에서 꺼낸 마지막 국물
밥 한술을 말아서 저녁으로 떼우는
눈물 어린 하루

쪽 방 사는 가난한 사람들
라면 국물 하나에 적시는 아픈 가슴
언제면 씻겨질까?

Tearful Ramen Soup

In the soup where ramen soup was simmered
A ramen is boiled and eaten as breakfast

In the remaining broth
A pack of udon needles is boiled and eaten as lunch
Into the last broth taken out of the refrigerator
Some rice is put and eaten as dinner
A tearful day

Poor people living in slice rooms
The painful heart wetted in just ramen broth
When will it be washed?

공룡의 사멸

발자국을 여문 돌로 만든 시간
해시계를 거꾸로 돌려야 밝혀질 공룡사멸의 원인
자연은 생성과 사멸의 수레바퀴를 끊임없이 돌린다
가장 낮은 것을 가장 높게 하고
가장 작은 것으로 가장 큰 것을 무너뜨리는
신神의 한 수가 작동되는 것인지
호기심이 두려움으로 바뀐다

눈에 보이지 않는 미세한 바이러스가
큰 공룡을 파멸시킨 존재일지 모른다
당시에는 백신도 약도 없었다

부패한 눈으로 신神을 쳐다볼 때마다
신神은 인간을 흔들어 놓았다
중세의 페스트
근자에 나타난 우한 코로나바이러스19
불안스레 허물어지기 쉬운 존재가 우리임을 절규한다

변종으로 쉽게 바뀌는 바이러스에게 배웠음인가?
때로는 신神의 후예였다가, 만물의 영장이었다가
미물보다 못하다고 스스로 가면을
자주 바꾸는 변덕꾸러기

Extinction of Dinosaurs

The cause of the extinction of dinosaurs that can be revealed only by turning the sundial backward
By the time that made footprints into hard stones
Nature constantly spins the wheel of creation and extinction
Changing the lowest into the highest and
Breaking the biggest with the smallest
A skill of God might work
Curiosity turns into fear

Microscopic viruses that are invisible to the eyes
Might be the being that ruined the big dinosaurs
There were no vaccines or drugs at the time.

Whenever humans I look at God with corrupt eyes
God shook humans
Pestis the Middle Ages
Wuhan coronavirus 19 that appeared recently
We scream that we are the beings that can easily collapse

Have they learned from viruses that easily turn into variants?
Sometimes they were descendants of God, other times they were the lords of the creation
They are men of mood who change the mask frequently
Believing that they are microbes

수백 년 동안 억눌린 양반에 대한 반항이
애환의 표출에 의지하여
단 하루라도 설움을 잊어버리고
자유롭고 싶을
탈춤 하나에 맡기는 인생
안동 하회 탈춤을 춘다

공룡은 탈춤을 출 수 없었다
풍부한 먹이가 모자라도
얼어붙는 빙하의 지표에서 살아남을 수 있는 가면을 쓰고
바이러스와 함께 춤을 추었는지 모른다

역사의 외진 끄트머리를 잡고 울었을
공룡의 마지막 비명
우주 어느 한쪽에서
아직 울려 퍼지는 퍼즐의 파장이 흐르고 있을 뿐이다

The rebellion against the nobles who have suppressed them for hundreds of years
Relies on the expression of sorrow
To forget the sadness for even a day
Wanting to be free
They leave their lives to mask dance only, and
Do Andong Hahoe mask dance

Dinosaurs could not do mask dance
Wearing a mask that enables them to survive on the surface of a frozen glacier
Even when there is not enough food
They might have danced with viruses

The last scream of dinosaurs
That should have cried holding the remote edge of history
At a side of the universe
Still resonating ripples of the puzzle are flowing.

싹이 나는 부지깽이

어머니는 매서운 연기를 마셔가며 시커멓게 눈물로 범벅 된 오늘을 태운다
산山에서 지게에 업혀 와 갈가리 찢겨
생존의 몸부림을 쳐도 소용없이
열반涅槃의 길로 접어든다
한 조각 남겨진 육신은 아궁이에 들락날락거리며 뜨거운 사랑을 연마하고 있다
때때로 재를 음식처럼 먹으며 갈증에 섞인 눈물을 흘리기도 했다

점점 더해가는 무딘 가슴에
눈물을 뺨에 흘리며
몸에 붙어있는 스트레스를 떼 내는 데 안간힘을 쓴다
한탄과 타령을 자리바꿈하고
그을음이 짙은 부엌에 하루를 건다

늙은이들은 청년기를 지나 유아기로 다시 돌아가 기저귀를 차고
패러독스의 글자 놀음을 하는 환상을 걸머지고 세상을 두려워한다

Sprouting Poker

My mother burns today covered with tears to become black while inhaling acrid smoke
Carried on the back from the mountain, torn to tatters
Regardless of struggles for survival
The firewood enters the path of Nirvana
A piece of the body that is left is polishing up the passionate love while going in and out of the furnace.
Sometimes I ate ashes as food and shed tears mixed with thirst.

Due to my heart that gradually becomes duller
Shedding tears on my cheek
I try hard to take off the stress attached to my body
After replacing lament with bewailing my lot
I bet one day for the soot-drenched kitchen

Elderly persons carry the illusion to go back to the infancy through adolescence, wear diapers,
And play with paradox letters and fear the world

말라버린 샘들
타버린 정열
어느 하나 생식본능마저 채울 수 없는 황량한 아궁이에는
꺼먼 입만 크게 벌리고 있다
뜻 없는 소리를 허공에 질러대면
치매라는 단어가 메아리 되어 쏟아진다

옴츠러든 아궁이에 땔감이 떨어지고
더는 쓸 곳 없는 부지깽이에 싹이 나는 청명절淸明節에
단비가 내린다

Dried springs
Burned passion
In a desolate furnace that cannot even fill in any reproductive instinct
Only the mouth is wide open.
When one shouts meaninglessly into the air
The word dementia pours as echoes

Firewood runs out in the shrunk furnace
On the Qīngmíng Festival day when the poker that cannot be used any more sprouts
Timely rain falls

하나일 수 없는

마음속에 숨겨 둔 사람을 그리워한들
넓은 고독의 바다를 건너
만날 수 있을지 없을지 모르는 혼돈
보고픔만 얄팍한 신앙처럼 떠돈다

사랑이 흔들릴 때
마음을 별빛으로 묶어둘 성좌는 어디에 있으며
별을 바라보는 그리움은 어느 지표에 있을까?
항상 꽉 찬 가슴인데 텅 빈 것 같아 허전하다

소녀의 가슴이 망울져 부풀어 오르듯
그대 향한 마음 풍선 되어
바람을 타고 하늘에 오르지만
줄을 잡은 손에서 벗어나지 못하고 길들어질 때
둘이 하나가 되었다고 느끼는 짧은 순간
기쁨도 한정이 된다

가끔, 풍선이 터지든가 아니면 줄을 놓아버리든가
자유가 말살되거나 원치 않는 자유를 누릴 수밖에 없는
주어진 운명이 아니던가?

Cannot Be One

Although I miss the person hidden in their heart
The chaos of not knowing if we can meet
By crossing the wide sea of solitude
Only longing floats like a shallow faith

Where is the constellation to which the heart will be tied with starlight,
When love is shaken?
At which surface of the earth is the longing to stare stars?
My heart is always full, but it feels empty because it seems empty

As with a girl's chest that swells up in lumps
My heart to you becomes a balloon
And rides the wind to ascend to the sky
When you are unable to get out of the hand holding the line and get tamed
To the brief moment when you feel that you two become one
Joy is limited, too

Sometimes, the balloon pops up or the string is released
Liberty is obliterated or undesired freedom cannot but be enjoyed,
Isn't it a given fate?

같은 침대에서 한 사람은 벽으로 돌아눕고
또 한 사람은 창틈으로 새어드는 별빛을 향해
불면의 밤을 지새우며
서로가 다른 세계로 접어드는 밤
비탄의 한숨 위에 그리움을 올려놓는다

In the same bed, one person turns to the wall
Another person faces towards the starlight that seeps through the window gap
Passing a sleepless night
The two persons enters different worlds from each other
They put longing on top of a sigh of grief

나그네의 슬픔

옥토를 떠나 살아야 할 나이
아무리 문빗장을 견고하게 잠가봐도
틈새에 들어오는 고독은 무섭다

밤에 별빛을 보고 즐거워해 본들
낮이면 폭양에
갈증으로 떨고 있다

추수 전에 떨어지는 씨알같이
자신에게 주어진 자리도 지키지 못한 채
세찬 바람 앞에 흩어져
정처 없이 떠도는 방황

흙으로 돌아갈 기억을 더듬는 티끌은
풍요에도 굶주림에도
한恨이 서린 춤을 추는
집시들의 플라멩코를 생각한다

Sorrow of a Wanderer

At the age to live off the fertile land
No matter how tightly locked the door bars
The solitude that enters through the gap is scary

Although delighted watching the starlight at night
In the daytime, due to the blazing sunlight
Is trembling with thirst

Like seeds falling before harvest
Not being able to keep the places given to them
Scattered in front of the strong wind
Aimlessly wandering here and there

The dust that traces the memory for going back to the dirt
Whether in abundance or in hunger
The dance laden with resentment
Thinks of the flamenco of the gypsy

장모님의 노랫소리

축복의 100세 고개 넘을 때까지
슬픔과 고통 속에서 보낸 한 세월
가기 싫은 집 떠나 요양원에 가야 했던 운명
현대판 고려장이 아니던가?
이유야 어떻든
한 어미는 열 자식 보살피며 키울 수 있으나
열 자식 다 해도 한 어머니 모시지 못하는 현실
세상 떠난 후 후회한들 무슨 소용 있을까?

세월이 흐를수록 모습은 희미해지나
더욱 그리워지는 어머니의 품속

과거를 잊어버리는 치매에도
나만 가면 반가워해 주시는 장모님
감사하다 말 한마디와 벅찬 가슴을
울음으로 대신하던 인자하신 분
휠체어에 앉아서도 나 위해 노래 불러주던 고운 마음
무엇으로 갚을까 눈물이 내 앞을 가로막는구나!
내일이면 눈 감을지
오늘이면 이별할지 조마조마한 마음
가눌 길 없다

Singing Voice of Mother-in-law

Until she crossed over the blessed pass of 100 years of age
The time spent in sorrow and pain
The fate of having to leave the house and go to the nursing home she did not want to go
Wasn't it a modern Goryeojang?
Whatever the reason was
Although one mother can care for and raise ten children,
The reality is that even ten children cannot support one mother
What is the use of regret after the mother left the world?

Although the appearance fades over time
I miss the bosom of my mother more and more

Despite her dementia that makes her forget the past
My mother-in-law is glad whenever I visit her
A benevolent woman who had been replacing
A word of thanks and overwhelming delight with crying
The sweetheart to sing for me even when she was sitting in a wheelchair
How can I pay back, tears stand in my way!

Whether she will close her eyes tomorrow
Or we will part today, the nervous feeling
Can never be controlled

신앙심 깊은 권사 팻말 가지고
하늘나라 가시면 주님의 우편에서
나 위하여 기도하실 테지
장모님의 노랫소리 아직도 내 귀에 쟁쟁하게 들리고 있다

With a sign of a deeply religious deaconess
If she goes to heaven, at the right side of the Lord
She will pray for me
The singing voice of my mother-in-law is still ringing in my ears.

슬픈 여운

공허한 마음에서 살아온 과거
육신을 잃어버린 빈 소라 껍데기에
별빛으로 채워보고
환상으로 채워봐도
손가락 사이로 빠져나가는 허황된 꿈일 뿐
이별이란 사랑의 꼬리가 퇴화하는 신기루였다

굽이쳐 흐르는 강물 위에
설레는 여운餘韻마저 띄워 보내는 혼백魂魄
싸늘한 빙판 위에 미끄러진다

순결이 후회의 무덤 속에 잠들면
상처는
또 다른 이에게 이전되는 슬픈 사실

무無에서 유有를 불러내는 창조의 힘이나
공허에서 불러내는 사랑의 힘이 위대하다 한들
슬픔이나 기쁨도
무엇 하나 소중하지 않은 것이 어디 있을까!

말없이 바라보는 눈빛만 봐도
슬픔 속에서 바라는 갈구를 미리 알고
위로를 마음에 가득 채워주는 손길이 그립다

Sad Afterglow

In the past I lived with a vacant mind
Although the empty conch shell that lost its body
Was filled with starlight
Or with fantasy
It was just a wild dream that slips through the fingers
Parting was a mirage in which the tail of love degenerates.

On the meandering river water
The spirit that floats even the afterglow that makes the heart flutter
Slips on the cold ice

When chastity fell asleep in the grave of regret
The wound
Is transferred to another, which is a sad fact

Even if the power of creation that calls out existence from naught
Or the power of love invoked from the void is great
Is sorrow or joy or whatsoever
Not precious?

Only after seeing the look of watching
Knowing the longing in sorrow in advance
The hand that fills my heart with comfort is what I miss

구토하는 승객

브레이크를 자주 밟는 버스 기사
중심을 잃고 바로 서는 오뚝이가 어지럽다
콩나물시루를 흔들어 공간을 없앤다

혼란스럽게 요동치는 승객의 울분
잃어버린 평정은 인내와 싸우며
체면이 등을 쓰다듬는다

다 꺼져버린 촛불에 밤은 깊어가고
소화되지 않는 연료가 토해내는 매연이 짙다

시달리는 버스 속에 구토 심한 탑승자들
종착역 가기 전에 중간중간 다 내리고
빈 버스만 정신없이 갈지자로 가고 있다

Vomiting Passenger

The bus driver who frequently steps on the brake
To the extent that the roly-poly toy that stands upright after losing balance is dizzy
Shakes the jar of bean sprouts to remove empty space

The resentment of passengers who are shaken chaotically
The lost composure fights patience
Face strokes the back

The night is getting deeper due to the candles that are all gone
The fumes spewed by the indigestible fuel are thick.

Severely vomiting passengers in the bus where they suffer
Get off the bus in here and there in middle before the bus goes to the last stop
Only the empty bus is going in zigzags

제4장 붓꽃으로 다가온 당신

Chapter IV
You Who came as an Iris

노랑나비

아침이슬 베어 문 프리지어에
노랑나비 한 마리 날개를 편다

피어나는 꽃
향기가 아름답다

날개 하나 밤을 덮고
남은 하나 낮을 덮는다

하늘을 다 안았다

상처 난 내 마음에
두 날개 접고
고요히 기도하는 노랑나비 한 마리

구름 걷히고 하늘 문이 열린다

Yellow Butterfly

On the freesia that holds one bite of morning dew
A yellow butterfly spread its wings

Blooming flower
The scent is beautiful

One wing covers the night
The remaining one covers the day

To embrace the entire sky

For my broken heart
Folded both wings
The yellow butterfly prays silently

The clouds lift and the door of the sky opens.

붓꽃으로 다가온 당신

안개 자욱이 피어오르는 호숫가
햇빛은 바쁘게 아침을 걷어내고
하늘 닮은 보랏빛 꽃봉오리를 흔들어 깨웁니다

풍성한 물감으로 채색된 풀꽃들
호수 속에 노니는 여유로운 물고기
당신의 캔버스에는 여름으로 가득 찼습니다

계절 따라 시든 꽃잎
한 잎 한 잎 떨어져
내 마음에 파문을 일으킬 때
그리움에 어우러진 풀벌레 소리가
방황하는 나를 위로해 줍니다

여름 지나 차가움이 엄습해
잎들이 흩어져
마지막 가랑잎 구르는 소리에도
당신의 숨결을 느끼게 됩니다

괴로운 세상 지나며 쓰러질 때
활짝 핀 붓꽃으로 다가와 고요히 웃으며
조심스레 손잡아 일으켜 주시던 손길
당신의 따뜻한 사랑이 나를 데우고 있습니다

You Who came to Me as an Iris

In the lakeside where mist rises densely
The sunlight busily clears the morning, and
Wakes up purple buds that resemble the sky by shaking

Grass flowers colored with rich paints
Relaxed fish strolling in the lake
Your canvas is full of summer

When petals withered according to the seasons
Fell one by one
To cause a stir in my heart
The sound of grass bugs mixed with longing
Comfort me who is wandering

As the cold sweeps over since summer has passed
The leaves are scattered
And even at the sound of the rolling last withered leaf
I feel Your breath

When I was falling while passing the painful world
Approached as a broad-blown iris, smiling quietly
You grasped my hand carefully to raise me
Your warm love is heating me

포도송이 익을 때

해맑은 가을입니다
검푸른 포도송이 주렁주렁 달렸습니다
축 처진 가지들은 괴로워도 불평하지 않습니다

잎들이 노랗게 변해도
익어 가는 포도알은
기쁨으로 여물어 갑니다

영이 육을 떠나는 순간까지
나 위해 조용히 기도하시던
어머니 모습이
포도송이와 함께 영글어 갑니다

어느덧 나도 포도송이 되어
주인의 손을 기다리고 있는데
가을은 점점 깊어가고 있습니다

(영천 강영진 별빛 포도마을에서)

When Clusters of Grapes Are Ripening

It is sunny autumn
The dark blue grape clusters are hanging in full bearing
The drooping branches do not complain although they are painful

Although the leaves turn yellow
The ripening grapes
Become ripe with joy

Until the moment the spirit leaves the flesh
Prayed quietly for me
Mother's figure
Grows ripe together with the clusters of grapes

I also became a cluster of grapes
Waiting for the master's hand
While autumn is getting deeper and deeper

(Oct. 15, 2020, at Yeongcheon Yousng Jin Kang's Starlight Vineyard)

종말의 꿈

몸속에 칩을 심으면
칩이 상대방 마음을 해독解讀하여
온 세상은 바벨탑 이전의 언어로 돌아가
서로 소통하겠지

꿈이 많으면 근심이 많은 법
칩을 바꾸어 가며
우리는 티끌의 바벨탑을 다시 쌓고 있다

언제 끝날지 모르고 달리기만 하는 문명의 기술

심장의 붉은 피는 검게 되고
서서히 멈추어 가는 호흡에
보라, 우리의 욕망조차 칩이 가지고 있어
관 뚜껑을 덮을 때가 도래하고 있구나

그 어린 양이
책에 여섯 번째의 책에 봉인을 뗄 때가 되었구나

나는 신神을 믿는다

Dream of Apocalypse

If chips are implanted in the bodies
The chips will decrypt the other person's mind
So that the whole world goes back to the language before the Tower of Babel
To communicate with each other

Those who have many dreams should also have many worries
Changing chips
We are rebuilding the Tower of Babel of dirt

The technology of civilization that only runs without knowing when to finish

As the red blood of the heart turns black,
The breathing slowly stops
And behold, the chip has even our desires
The time to close the lid of the coffin is coming

The time for the young lamb
To unseal the sixth book has come

I believe in God

노란 밤

밤하늘에 떠 있는 달이
구름 뒤에 숨는다
내 얼굴이 낯선 모양이다

찾아온 바람이 다독이는 소리에
구름 사이로 살짝 얼굴을 내민다
어머니 치맛자락 뒤에 숨은 어린아이도
슬그머니 얼굴을 내민다

달빛 내리는 밤이면
달맞이꽃이 되어
흐르는 피아노 선율에 올라
노오란 꽃잎 활짝 열고
그대를 맞이한다

Yellow Night

The moon in the night sky
Hides behind clouds
Probably my face is unfamiliar to the moon

At the consoling sound of the wind that visited
The moon shows its face a little between the clouds
The little child hiding behind the skirt hem of his mother
Furtively shows his face

At every moonlit night
I become an evening primrose,
Ride on the flowing piano melody
With yellow petals open wide
And greet you

염원念願의 밤

외로운 반딧불이 하나
밤하늘에
별이 되어 깜박입니다

당신의 신비한 문을 열고
영롱한 빛으로
거기서 나도 함께 반짝이고 싶습니다

창가에 별빛 내리는 날이면
조용히 타오르는 그리움에
당신을 사랑하지 않을 수 없습니다

Night of Aspirsation

A lonely firefly
In the night sky
Became a star and blinks

I wish to open your mysterious door
With a bright light
And blink there together with you

On the day when the starlight falls on the window
Because of the quietly burning longing
I cannot but love you

시련에 피는 꽃

내가 걸어온 길 어제 같아 빠르기만 하다
낯설고 험한 길 원망 없이 왔건만
지치고 고단해도 참아내며 이룬 욕망
허물어지는 모래성처럼 부질없다

어두운 길섶에서 어찌할 바 모를 때
외로이 흘리는 눈물을 닦아 주던 손길
내 마음 깊은 곳에 뿌려놓은 사랑의 씨앗

입에서 나오는 사소한 언어들이
가시가 되지 않고
인자한 입술로
감화의 향기를 뿜어내게 되기를 원한다

쓰라리고 아픈 상처 가눌 수 없을 때도
고초苦楚당한 주님 얼굴 바라보면
절망에도, 죽음에도 사라지는 두려움

육신에서 영혼이 떠난다 해도
열락悅樂의 정원에서 피어날 꽃
믿음의 배를 타고
덧없는 세상 지나 영원의 문으로 들어갈
당신과 나

Flowers Blooming in Ordeals

The way I have walked is only fast as it is like yesterday
Although I came the unfamiliar and rugged way without resentment
The desire achieved while enduring even when I was exhausted and tired
Is vain like a crumbling sandcastle

When I did not know what to do at a dark roadside
The hand that wiped away the tears shed lonelily
Was the seed of love sown deep in my heart

I want the trivial languages coming out of the mouth
Not to not become thorns
But with benevolent lips
To spout the scent of influence

Even when I cannot manage my sore and painful wounds
If I look at the face of Jesus who suffered hardships
Fears disappears even in despair and death

Even if the soul leaves the body
Flowers will bloom in the garden of joy
You and I
Will ride on the boat of faith
To pass through the uncertain world and enter the door of eternity

당신만을

봄의 손길에 부드럽게 된 흙은
품었던 생명을 분만하고
풀꽃들이 봉오리를 열 때
솟구치는 그리움이 여인을 동산으로 인도한다

이슬에 젖은 여인의 발목을 본 신神은 그냥 두지 않았다
얼마나 사랑했기에 무덤까지 왔을까!
무덤의 돌문을 열어 죽음을 쫓아내고
빈 무덤을 지키던 메신저가 부활의 소식을 전하는 순간
슬픔이 몰려왔던 여인의 가슴은 환희와 감사로 부풀었다

돌아오는 길
동산지기인 줄 알았던 낯선 이가 사랑하는 사람일 줄이야!
사랑하는 이의 눈길이나 마음이 나에게만 머물기를 바라는
갈망에 젖은 여인

목을 축일 수 있는 한마디의 말
자신의 이름을 불러주는 소리에 끝난 슬픔
짓이겨진 포도송이에서 나오는 포도주보다 진한 환희였다

Only You

The soil softened by the hand of spring
Gives birth to the life it had
When the grass flowers open their buds
Soaring longing leads the woman to the garden

God who saw the ankle of a woman wet with dew did not leave her alone.
How much she loved to come to the grave!
After opening the stone door of the tomb to drive out death
At the moment the messenger who had been guarding the empty tomb delivered the news of the resurrection
The woman's heart, which had been filled with sorrow, was swollen with joy and gratitude.

On the way back
She realizes that the stranger who seemed to be a gardener was her beloved!
Wanting the eyes and heart of her beloved to stay only on her
The woman wet with longing

A word that she can soothe her throat
Sadness ended at the sound of calling her name
It was a deeper delight than the wine coming from the crushed cluster of grapes.

아픔과 눈물로 범벅이 된 사랑이라도
저버릴 수 없는 사연을 간직한 채
고스란히 마음을 바쳐
한 사람을 가슴에 두고 섬긴다는 것은
모든 것을 외면하고 하나의 신神만을 경배하는 것과 같았다

사랑은 인내의 밭에서 키워내는 진실의 열매
비록 그이의 기억 끝에 머물러 있다 해도
품에 안은 진실로서 스스로를 지키고 있다

Even a love filled with pain and tears
Preserving a story that cannot be forsaken
And giving the heart completely
To serve one person in her heart
Was like worshiping only one deity disregarding everything.

Love is the fruit of truth cultivated in the field of patience
Even if she stays at the end of his memory
She was protecting herself with the truth embraced in her arms

시들지 않는 장미

해마다 다가오는 봄을
새롭게 느끼는 것은
황량한 겨울을 지냈기 때문이다

날마다 만나도 또 보고픈 것은
숱한 오해와 질투를 녹여내는 당신이기에
자꾸만 곁에 있고 싶다

가슴에 심어놓은 붉은 장미 한 송이
저녁노을 불태우는 날이 되어도
내 가슴에 붉게 피어오르는 당신이 아름답다

천년이고 만년이고
지지 않는 한 송이 꽃
영원의 세계에서 날마다 새롭게 피어날
아름다운 당신

A Rose That Does Not Wither

The reason why spring that comes every year
Is felt new is that
The desolate winter was undergone

The reason why I miss you even if I meet you every day
Is that you melt countless misunderstandings and jealousy
Making me want to be at your side

A red rose planted in my heart
Even the day to burn the evening glow has come
You, who bloom red in my heart, are beautiful

Whether thousand years or ten thousand years
A piece of flower that does not fall
You, who are beautiful,
Will bloom every day in the world of eternity

하얀 크로커스

방 한 칸 빌려 공부하던
독일의 눈 덮인 정원에
하얀 눈을 뚫고 나오는
꽃대 하나가
허리를 펴고
살며시 주위를 살핀다

하얀 크로커스꽃 한 송이 웃음이 예쁘다

반갑게 살펴보는 독일 할머니의 얼굴에 주름이 펴진다

White Crocus

When I rented a room and studied
In Germany, at the snowy garden
Coming out through white snow
A flower stalk
Straightened its back
Gently looked around

A white crocus flower with a pretty smile

The wrinkles of the German elderly woman, who was gladly looking at the flower, were smoothed

마음에 쓰는 편지

지리산 숲속을 헤치고 산에 오르면
안개를 두르고 있는 정상
풀 끝이 바람에 흔들리기 전
이슬을 붓끝에 묻혀 편지를 쓴다

서툰 마음으로 쓴 글
한 구절씩 또르르 굴러 감격의 눈물 되어
그녀의 치마폭에 떨어진다

아침에 찾아온 햇빛이
어둠에서 헤매던 짐승 발자국을 쓸어내면
나는 오늘도 내일도 정지된 시간 속에서
끊임없이 편지를 쓴다

그녀의 검은 눈동자에 아름다운 꽃이 피고
무지개를 등에 업은 골짜기에
흐르는 물소리가 청명하게 울려 나올 때
산새들도 함께 노래한다

우리는 반쪽 마음을 서로 맞추어 하나로 만든다
붓끝에 시간이 마르고 요염한 침묵이 시작된다

A Letter Written to the Heart

When climbed Jirisan Mountain after cutting through the forests
The summit surrounded by fog appears
Before the end of the grass is shaken by the wind
I smear the tip of a brush with dew to write a letter

A writing written with a clumsy mind
The phrases roll round and round one by one to become tears of effervescence
And fall on her skirt

When the sunlight that came in the morning
Swept the footprints of beasts that wandered in the dark
Today, tomorrow, etc. in stopped time
I write letters unceasingly

When beautiful flowers bloomed in her black pupils
And the sound of flowing water resonates clearly
In the valley carrying a rainbow on its back
Mountain birds also sing together

We put the half hearts together to make one heart
Time dries up at the tip of the brush, and a dry and fascinating silence begins.

당신 곁에

나는 알아요
초라한 들풀에도 작고 예쁜 꽃을 피우게 하는
당신이 누구신지 나는 알아요

부드러운 손길로 안개와 구름을 만드신 당신
몸과 마음이 나약해서 눈물 흘릴 때
흰 눈같이 깨끗게 하심을 나는 알아요

물을 돌같이 여문 얼음으로 만드시는
차가운 분노도 알아요
나는 당신의 얼굴을 외면할 수 없어요

사랑이라는 단어에만 현혹되어
망상의 밤을 헤매며
쾌락의 유방을 빨고
주린 욕정의 이불을 덮고 잠들어
허무하게 사그라지는 재[灰]가 되지 않을 거예요

자연의 탄생과 사라짐을 주관하시는 당신
나의 손을 잡고 함께 길을 가는 걸음마다
감사하는 마음으로
당신 곁에서 항상 머물 거예요

By Your Side

I know
The one who makes even shabby wild grass bloom small and pretty flowers
I know who You are

You who made fog and clouds with a gentle touch
When we cry because the body and mind are weak
I know You clean us like white snow

I also know Your cold anger
That turns water into ice hard as stone
I cannot turn away from Your face

I will not be deluded by only the word love
To wander through the night of delusions
Such the breast of pleasure
Fall asleep under the blanket of hungry lust
And become ashes that disappear in vain

You who preside over the birth and disappearance of nature
At every step to walk along the road together with me holding my hand
With a thankful heart
I will always stay by Your side

백조의 걸음걸이

비틀걸음 걷는 아기
보고 있던 백조도 뒤뚱 걸음 걷는다

철커덕 물 위에 내려앉는 불안한 백조
두서너 발걸음에 앉으려다 넘어지는 아기

제각기 미숙하게 보이지만
힘겹게 뚫어내는 고난

지나간 옛일인 듯
나날이 성숙하고 의젓한 모습에 행복감이 깃든다

Swan's Gait

A baby walks with tottering steps
The swan that was looking it also walks with tottering steps

The unstable swan that settles on the water with rattling
The baby who falls down while trying to sit after a couple of steps

Although they look immature
They struggle through hardship

As if that was past history
A feeling of happiness indwells at the maturing and dependable appearances seen day by day.

할슈타트

신神은 알프스 산자락에
천상의 아름다움을 수채화로 그리고
그 위에 시詩를 썼다
'할슈타트'

데칼코마니를 그려내는 호수
여기 위대한 음악가가 나타나
'송어'를 5중주곡으로 작곡할 때
거룩하도록 순결한 천사들의 노래가
잔잔한 호수 위에 흐른다

백합보다 더 아름다운 할슈타트
태양의 모든 영광을 구름 위에 얹어
아름다운 광채를 발하게 하고
산은 하얀 눈으로 신비의 꽃을 피운다

지성소 같은 소금 마을은
사랑의 언약궤를 품은 듯 성스럽기까지 하다

내 사랑하는 자와 영원히 쉬고 싶은 이곳
더이상 한 걸음도 옮기기 싫은
꿈을 안겨주는 소금 마을
고향보다 그리움이 더 짙다

Hallstatt

At the food of the Alps, God
Painted the heavenly beauty in watercolors
And wrote a poem on it.
'Hallstatt'

When at the lake that draws décalcomanie
Appears a great musician
To compose "Trout" as a quintet
The song of angels who are pure to be holy
Flows over the calm lake

Hallstatt, which is more beautiful than a lily
After putting all the glory of the sun on the clouds
To make the clouds emit beautiful luster
The mountain blooms mysterious flowers with white snow.

The salt village, which is like the Holy of Holies
Is even sacred as if it harbors the ark of the covenant of love

This place where I want to rest forever with my loved one
From where I do not want to take even a step further
The salt village that gives dreams
Is longed for more than my hometown

아름다운 블레드 호수에서

병사들의 나팔소리 사라져
고요가 깃든 성城에 군주들의 위엄은 온데간데없고
흔적이라도 놓칠세라 붙들고 있는 나그네들
성城을 중심으로 뻗어나던 도시조차 보이질 않는다

슬로베니아에서 만난 블레드 성城
알프스산맥의 만년설이 해산한 호수에서
계절마다 불어오는 바람을
절벽 위에 서서
온몸으로 맞는 작은 성城
동화 속 신비의 호수를 내려다본다

천년이 넘도록 지켜온 아름다운 자태
세월에 허물어지고 퇴색되는 게 아름다움이지만
블레드 호수는 변함없는 당신 마음 같아
아름다움이 가득하다

고통의 눈물과 환희로 채워진
순결한 가슴을 드러내는 섬
성모승천성당이 있어 하늘에 행복을 쌓고 있다

At the Beautiful Lake Bled

After the sound of the soldiers' trumpets disappeared
In the castle where silence indwells, the dignity of the monarchs cannot be found
Travelers are holding traces in fear of missing them
Even the city that stretched out centering around the castle cannot be seen

Castle Bled that was found in Slovenia
The winds that blow every season
From the lake where the perpetual snow of the Alps delivered a child
Hit the entire body of the small castle
Standing on the cliff
To overlook the mysterious lake in a fairy tale

A beautiful figure that has been preserved for over a thousand years
Although beauty collapses and fades over time
Lake Bled is like your unchanging heart
And is full of beauty

In the island that reveals a pure heart
Filled with tears of pain and joy
Is the Cathedral of Holy Mother Ascension to build happiness in the sky.

아직,
노를 저어 건너지 못한 호수
당신의 섬에 닿아
사랑이 있고 평화가 깃드는 아름다운 성城을 지어
호수에 별빛 내리는 날이면 은물결로 시詩를 읊고
낮이면 뭉게구름 한 아름 가져와 꿈으로 엮어
석양이 깃들면 당신의 섬에 올라
하루의 기쁨을 속삭이고 있다

Yet,
The lake has not been crossed by pulling on the oars
After reaching your island
A beautiful castle where there is love and peace indwells was built
To compose poems with silvery water on days when the starlight falls on the lake
Bring an armful of cumulus clouds during the daytime to weave dreams
Climb your island when the sunset falls
To whisper the joy of the day

무너진 교회에서

가난한 독일 유학 시절 오고 싶던 베를린
43년 지나서 찾아와보니 폭격에 무너진
빌헬름 교회가 보인다
과거에 입은 상흔 그대로
통일기념교회가 세월 속에서 몸부림친다

무너질 마음과 헐어버릴 육체의 시련에서도
순결한 마음으로
참된 모습 그대로 설 수 있는 그대가 장하다

어둡던 지난밤, 가식의 침실에서 벗어나
햇빛 드는 6시
진실의 갑옷으로 무장한 그대
브란덴부르크 문 위에 올라
네 마리 말이 이끄는 '승리의 콰드리'를 타고
아픈 상처 치유하며 위로하던 주님 앞으로
하늘 높이 오르면
온전한 빌헬름 교회는 찬연한 빛을 발하리라

(2019년 11월 14일 독일 베를린에서)

At the Collapsed Church

Berlin to where I wanted to come during the days in poverty of studying in Germany
I came 43 years later, and I see
Wilhelm Church, which collapsed due to bombing
With the scars made in the past as they are
The Unification Memorial Church struggles in times

Even with the mind that will crumble and the trials of the body that will be torn down
With a pure heart
You who can stand in the true figure as it is are admirable

Last night, which was dark, after getting out of the bedroom of pretense
At 6 o'clock when the sun streamed into the room
You were armed with the armor of truth
If you climbed on the Brandenburg Gate
Ride the 'Quadriga of Victory' pulled by four horses
And ascend high in the sky
To the front to the Lord who was comforting while healing painful wounds
The intact Wilhelm Church emit brilliant light

허물어진 장벽

나눔의 셈만 계산하는 자여!
오, 단절의 벽이여!
그리움과 비애를 벽에 그려 놓은 수많은 사연
베를린 장벽이 동서에 샌드위치 맨이 되지 않았던가?

비밀경찰, 학살, 독재
애통의 울음마저 막아버린
그 너머로 알릴 수 없는 배후의 잔인함이 두려웠었지!

장벽 위에 떨어질
같은 구름에서 내리는 빗방울들
하나는 동東으로
하나는 서西로 나누어져 흘러내렸던 몸뚱어리
슬픈 울음의 눈물과 함께 허옇게 늙어 가지 않았나

28년 동안 조심스레 반성의 물결은 덧셈을 가르쳐
갇힌 고통에서 해방된 베를린 장벽
허물어 버린 장벽의 흔적 앞에서
나그네는 부러운 마음에 눈시울을 적신다

(2019년 11월 14일 독일 베를린에서)

Demolished Barrier

Those who only calculate the amount of sharing!
Oh, the wall of severance!
Numerous stories of longing and sadness drawn on the wall
Didn't the Berlin Wall become a sandwich man between the east and west?

Secret police, slaughter, dictatorship
Blocked even the cry of mourning
The cruelty behind the wall that could not be informed across the wall was fearful!

The raindrops falling from the same cloud
That will fall on the barrier
One to the east
The other to the west, the body that was divided when flowing down
Grew old to become white with the tears of sad crying, didn't it?

For 28 years, the wave of self-reflection carefully taught addition
The Berlin Wall freed from the pain of being confined
In front of the traces of the demolished barrier
The traveler wets the eye-lids with envy.

(22 March 2020; 14 November 2019 in Berlin, Germany)

프라우엔교회

시민의 품으로 돌아온 교회
30년 종교전쟁에 헐뜯겨도
돌 하나 버리지 않고 모아둔 정성

저금통에 모아둔 고사리손의 성의
한 끼의 빵을 아낀 여인
노동의 대가를 십일조로 바치던 노동자들
작은 헌납들이 모여
드레스덴에 바로크 양식의 교회가 섰다

세계를 뒤흔들 부패에 반기를 들었던
종교개혁을 일으킨 용기를 전설처럼 이어갈
시민들의 자랑스런 자부심에
프라우엔 교회가 재건되었다

영적인 변혁에 앞장선 말틴 루터의 고향에서
오르간을 연주하던 바흐의 기분은 어떠했을까?
아름다운 돔을 쳐다보는 드레스덴 시민들
시민의 품으로 돌아온 프라우엔교회
과거와 현실에서 함께 살고 있다

(2019년 11월 14일 독일 베를린에서)

Frauen Church

The church that has returned to the arms of citizens
Although torn out in the 30-year religious war
The devotion that gathered everything without throwing away even a single stone

The sincerity of the cute little hand collected in the piggy bank
Women who saved the bread for one meal
Workers who gave tithes from the price of their labor
Small donations gathered
So that the Baroque church was built in Dresden

Thanks to the proud pride of the citizens
That will succeed like a legend the courage that initiated the Reformation
In revolt against corruption that would shake the world
Frauen Church was rebuilt

In the hometown of Martin Luther, who took the lead in spiritual transformation
How did Bach feel while playing the organ?
Dresden citizens looking at the beautiful dome
Frauen Church that has returns to citizens' arms
Is living both in the past and in reality

(March 23, 2020, November 14, 2019 in Berlin, Germany)

군주의 행렬

슈탈호프 외벽에는
작센의 역대 왕들의 행렬이 시작된다
군주의 무덤을 향해 전열을 가다듬고
101미터 모자이크 그림 밖에서 기다리고 있는 낭떠러지로
용감하게 가고 있다
25,000개의 도자기 타일 위에서 미끄러진 권력
군주의 무덤이 될 20세기가 기다리고 있는 줄 모르고
말발굽 소리가 요란하다

왕들의 권력은
신神으로부터 부여받은 것이라고 생각했을
왕권신수설에 종교까지 끌어 들인다
권력은 백성의 딸들을 데려와 요리사나 제빵 기술자로
농부의 올리브밭을 착취하고
노예로 만들 것을 몰랐던 피지배자들
이미 신神의 품을 벗어난 후회
그들의 신神은 응답하지 않았다

'군주의 행렬'을 쳐다보는 여행자
지금도 세계 곳곳에
군주의 계승자가 남아있는 시각이 외롭다

(2019년 11월 14일 독일 베를린에서)

Procession of Monarchs

On the outer wall of Stahlhof
The procession of the kings of Saxony of many generations begins
After bracing up toward the tomb of monarchs
To the cliff waiting outside the 101 meter mosaic painting
They are bravely going
The power slipped on 25,000 porcelain tiles
Not knowing that the 20th century, which will become the tomb of monarchs, is waiting
The sound of horses' hoofs is loud

To the theory of the Divine Right of Kings, which thought
That the power of kings was
Given by God, even region is induced
The ruled people who did not know that
The power would take the daughters of the people and use them as into cooks and bakers,
Exploit farmers' olive field, and
Make the farmers into slaves
Regretted that they already got out of the arms of God
Their deity did not respond

Travelers looking at the 'procession of monarchs'
Even now, all over the world
The view of the monarch's successors remaining is lonely

(March 23, 2020, November 14, 2019 in Berlin, Germany)

프라하의 밤

신神의 손으로 빚어낸 프라하
붉은 지붕 아래서 태어난 사람들의 열정이
천년고도에서 살아 숨 쉬고 있다

블타바강 사이를 두고 서 있는 그대와 나
별처럼 쏟아지는 그리움에 끓어오르는 정情으로
프라하의 밤이 시작되면 카를교 위에서 만나자

카를교 위
성 요한 네포무크에 고해성사를 하는
보헤미안 왕비의 부조浮彫된 치맛자락을 만지면
사랑이 이뤄진다는 주술에
속는 줄 알면서 만져보는
불쌍한 나그네들
우리 서로 만나는 미소가 환희의 눈물에 적셔
하나의 숨결로 이어갈 신神의 은총恩寵이
프라하의 밤을 아름답게 빛내는 노래가 되어
내 마음을 앞질러 간다

Night in Prague

Prague made with the hands of God
The passion of people born under the red roof
Is alive and breathing at the thousand-year old city

You and I standing across the Vltava River
With the affection that boils due to the longing that pours like stars
Let us meet on the Charles Bridge when the night in Prague has begun

On Charles Bridge
Because of the charm that love will come true
If the person touches the hem of the skirt carved in relief of the bohemian queen
Who confesses her sins to Saint John of Nepomuk
Poor travelers
Who touch the aforementioned hem despite that they know they are deceived
The smiles of us when we meet are soaked in the tears of joy
The grace of the gods that will lead to one breath
Becomes a song that brightens up the night in Prague, and
Goes ahead of my mind

아름다운 야경을 보고
별빛이 내려오기가 부끄러워 망설일 때
나는 고요히 그대 이름 부르며
흐르는 강물 위에 사랑의 종이배를 띄워 보낸다

(2019년 11월 15일 체코 프라하에서)

Looking at the beautiful night view
When the starlight is ashamed and hesitates to come down
I quietly call your name
And send a paper boat of love on the flowing river water

(March 27, 2020, November 15, 2019 in Prague, Czech Republic)

프라하 성城

부富와 권력, 적의 공격과 약탈, 방어를 버무려 세운 성곽
천년의 세월이 피곤타

르네상스에 내어준 성城의 정체성
예술의 낭만적 조류가 담을 넘어
성 비투스 성당의 영혼과 육체에 신비한 매력을 가진
신권과 왕권을 둘러싼지 수 세기

목숨과 명분을 바꾸게 될
30년 종교전쟁의 도화선에 불붙인
보헤미안 총독의 방을
성城은 증언을 하고 있다

왕국과 종교까지 품은 프라하 성城에서
나는 구석구석을 카메라로 시간을 붙잡아 모았다

성城은 자신의 몸에서 기억을 끄집어내어
시간 위를 걸어가는 발걸음을 잡고
되돌아갈 수 없는 인간들에게
영과 육의 세계를 연결하는 사다리를 보여준다

Prague Castle

A fortress built by mixing wealth and power, enemy's attacks and plunders, and defense
Is tired of thousand years

The identity of the castle given to the Renaissance
The romantic tide of art crossed the wall
And surrounded the soul and body of St. Vitus Cathedral and
The divine right and royal authority with a mysterious charm for several centuries

The castle testifies
The room of the Bohemian governor
Who ignited the fuse of the 30-year religious war
That would exchange life with cause

In Prague Castle, which embraces the kingdom and even religion
I grabbed and collected time with my camera from every nook and corner.

The castle draws out memories from its own body
To hold the steps walking on time
And shows ladder that connects the spiritual and physical worlds
To humans who cannot go back

차디찬 겨울에
저 유명한 프라하의 봄을 맞으며
세월에 풍화되어 헐어져 가는 성城은 몸을 일으켜
석조 문화로 꽃피운 영욕榮辱의 발자취를 보여주고 있다

(2019년 11월 15일 체코 프라하에서)

In the cold winter
Greeting the famous spring of Prague
The castles that have weathered over time and is being dilapidates raises its body
To shows the traces of glory and shame blossomed with stone culture.

(March 28, 2020, November 15, 2019 in Prague, Czech Republic)

성스러운 호수에서

어떤 중력도 미치지 않는 신神의 공간에서 내려온
아름답고도 성스러운 고요한 호수
사랑하는 이의 마음 같아
나그네의 마음은 기쁨에 파르르 떨고 있다

천사들의 하얀 연회복宴會服 끝자락이
황홀감에 취하여
당신의 호수에 닿을 듯 말 듯
신神이 내린 찬란한 영광이
당신의 순결을 환희에 눈을 뜨게 하는구나

사랑하는 자여!
이곳에서 하늘을 보라!
비행기가 지나간 구름 자국이
세포 속 염색체 같다는 그 재치才致있던 말
지금은 가고 없는 옛 스승의 고향 하늘에서
다시 보게 되는구나

나그네 된 나
할슈타트 호수에 신비롭게 피어나는 구름이 되어
호수가 된 당신을 안고
환희의 꿈을 꾸고 있구나

(2019년 11월 22일 오스트리아 할슈타트에서)

At the Sacred Lake

Came down from the space of the deity not affected by any gravity
The beautiful yet sacred lake
Is like the heart of the beloved
The traveler's heart is trembling with joy.

The edges of the white banquet dress of the angels
Are intoxicated with ecstasy
And became to almost come into contact with your lake
The splendid glory given by God
Makes your purity feel joy for the first time

My beloved!
Look at the sky from here!
The witty words that the mark of airplane that passed through the clouds
Was like chromosomes in a cell
I see again
In the sky of the hometown of the old teacher who is now gone

I who have become a traveler
Became a cloud mysteriously formed above Lake Hallstatt
Embracing you who became the lake
And is dreaming of joy

(March 29, 2020, November 22, 2019 in Hallstatt, Austria)

폼페이 성城의 슬픔

주여, 아시아 먼 곳에서 들었던 말들이 사실인지
도마보다 심한 의심을 안고 여기에 왔습니다

일찍 당신이 보여준
환락의 소돔 성城을 못 잊어
뒤돌아보다 소금 기둥이 된 롯의 아내처럼
도자 가마에 들어간 폼페이 성城은
용광로보다 뜨거운 불길로도 태우지 못한 쾌락이
참혹한 화석으로 구워져 있습니다

완전히 소성燒成이 되지 못하고 쇠퇴衰退의 길로 치달은 향락을
의심의 손으로 더듬어 봅니다

요즘 세상에는 타락한 정보가 시공간을 넘어
인터넷을 타고 퍼트려지는 빠른 손놀림은
젊은이를 녹슬게 합니다

내가 사는 대도시에 의인 열 명도 없는지
이미 이곳에 역병이 일어나
불안하게 사람들을 흔들고 있습니다

Sorrow of Pompeii Castle

Lord, whether the words I heard from far away in Asia are true,
I came here with more suspicion than Thomas.

Like Lot's wife who became a pillar of salt after looking back
Because she could not forget the Sodom Castle of joy
You showed earlier,
In the Pompeii Castle, which entered the ceramic kiln
The pleasure that could not be burned even with the flames hotter than the furnace
Is baked as a horrific fossil.

The pleasure that was not completely calcined but rushed to the path of decline
I grope with my hand of suspicion

In these days, corrupt information goes beyond time and space.
And quickly spread through the Internet by fast hands
To rust young people

Probably there are less than ten righteous people in the big city where I live
A plague was already developed here
To shake people making them anxious

늙은이들은 조여오는 면역결핍 쇠사슬에 죽어가고
젊은이들은 어두운 방에 갇혀 떨고 있습니다

독소를 빨아들인 뿌리는 썩고
꽃잎이 떨어져도 맺지 못할 열매
언제 태어나
언제 죽을지 모르며 쾌락만을 좇는 어리석은 인간의 한계를
폼페이 성城은 증언하고 있습니다

Old people are dying due to the tightening chains of immune deficiency
And young people are locked up in dark rooms and are trembling there

The roots that absorbed toxins rot
Even if petals fall, no fruit can be borne
The limitation of foolish man who pursues only pleasure
Not knowing when to be born
Or when to die
Is testified by Pompeii Castle

제5장 참회懺悔의 장

Chapter V
The Penitentiary Chapter

장마

하늘을 지나다 벼락 맞은 구름이
아픔을 무릅쓰고 번개를 안았다

스승을 팔아먹은 가룟 유다의 피는 황금색이었다
대가로 받는 상은
올가미를 걸어야 하는 자살의 멍에였다

무색의 비가 그칠 줄 모르고 내려도
씻지 못한 마음
구부러진 입에서 나오는 두 날 가진 날카로운 칼
유전자가 수천 대를 이어가며
흙탕물에 떠내려가고 있다

무지개는 빛을 산란散亂 하지 못한 채
기력을 잃고
혈관에서 썩는 냄새가
장마를 타고 뚝뚝 떨어진다

Rainy Season

Clouds hit by lightning while passing through the sky
Embraced lightning despite the pain

The blood of Judas Iscariot, who sold his teacher, was golden.
The prize he received in return
Was a suicide yoke on which a noose should be hung

Even though the colorless rain falls unceasingly
The heart could not be washed
A sharp knife with two blades coming out of a bent mouth
The gene of it has been passed through several thousand generations
While floating down in muddy water

Unable to scatter the light, the rainbow
Lost energy
The smell of rotting in the veins
Falls in the rainy season

닭울기 전

칼로 귀를 베어 땅에 떨어지게 해도 풀리지 않는 성품
곡선은 모난 직선을 품을 수 있어도
직선은 곡선을 품을 수 없다

바깥 뜰 모닥불 옆에 앉아 관망하고 있을 때 날씨가 추웠다
명분과 실리의 진흙탕 사이를 오가며 계산을 한다
두려움이 세 번이나 부인否認하게 한다
섬기며 사랑해온 사람을 모른다고 부인否認하는 것이 답이기 때문이다

닭이 울었다 가슴이 아린다

당신 속에 빛나는 별 하나만 보고 걸어온 길
주위 사람들은 부러워하지만
낮에도 어둠을 만나 더듬기를 밤과 같이하는 욕망
부정不正한 일일수록 자라나는 호기심에
진실은 위선에 쫓겨나고
어둠에 싸인 별빛처럼 점점 사라지는 언약에
무너지는 마음은 상처가 깊다

Before the Cock Crows

The nature that is not loosened even when the ear was cut to fall to the ground
Although curves can embrace angular straight lines
Straight lines cannot embrace curves

When watching sitting by a bonfire in the garden outside, it was cold
Calculate while moving back and forth between the causes and the mire of and practical interests
Fear makes me deny as many as three times
Because the answer is to deny that I don't know the person I have been serving and loving

The cock crowed, I have heartburn

The path I walked seeing only the star shining star in you
Although people around me envy
The desire to meet the darkness even during the day and grope like the night
Due to curiosity that grows more for unjust affairs
The truth is expelled by hypocrisy
Due to the covenant that fades away like a starlight wrapped in darkness
The collapsing heart is deeply wounded

몇 번이고 당신을 부인하는 변형된 사랑은
질투, 이별, 배신으로 끈적거린다

고요한 묵상 속에 어찌할 바 모르는 회한의 통곡으로
으스러지는 육체가 원소로 환원되는 환상을 본다

닭 울음이 들린다.
이미 새벽이다

The deformed love to deny you over and over again
Is sticky with jealousy, parting, and betrayal

In silent meditation, with the wailing of overwhelming remorse
I see the illusion that the shattered body is reduced to elements

I hear the cock crows
It is already dawn

무릎을 꿇고

찻잔에 고생이 담겨도 고운 마음 함께 넣어
서로 위로하며 마실 때
안개비 걷히고
지표에 꽃이 피는 아름다운 날이 되어
은밀히 흐르는 당신의 강물에 잠기고 있습니다

사랑의 중력이 유혹의 원심력보다 더 크기 때문에
나를 밀어내지 못하고
차지도 덥지도 않은 비굴한 중용中庸의 옷을 벗고서
당신을 사랑합니다

골고다 산상의 십자가 아래
새들이 지저귀면
층층나무에 피어나는 꽃송이 들고
나는
당신에게 이 한 몸 바칩니다

After Kneeling

Even if the hardship is contained in the teacup, after putting a heart of gold also
When we drink tea while consoling each other
The misty rain stops
They day becomes beautiful with flowers blooming on the ground surface
And I am immersed in Your secretly flowing river water

Because the gravity of love is greater than the centrifugal force of temptation
I cannot push me away
I take off the clothes of moderation, which is neither cold nor hot,
And love You

Under the cross on the Mount Golgotha
When birds are tweeting
Carrying the flowers blooming on the dogwood
I
I dedicate my body to You

따라나선 좁은 길

모퉁이를
굽이굽이 돌아 나온 길
노인은 잠시 등을 펴서 돌아본다

제 몫을 다한 꽃잎들이 떨어져
발아래 구른다
미래보다 과거가 눈부시다

눈가에 맺힌 노을이 영롱한 빛을 낼 때
태양도 허리 굽혀
조용히 서산마루에 몸을 기댄다

어둠 위에 펼쳐질 찬연한 나라 향해
무거운 형틀 걸머지고 가셨던
비아 돌로 로사의 좁은 길을
노인은 아무 말 없이 따라나선다

A Narrow Road That Was Followed

After winding around the corner
The road appeared
The old man stretches his back for a while to look back

The petals that held up their end fell and
Roll under his feet
The past is more dazzling than the future

When the glow of the setting sun formed around the eyes shines brightly
Even the sun bends down
To quietly lean on the peak of the western mountain

Toward a bright country that will spread out above the darkness
The narrow road of Via Dolorosa he went
Carrying the heavy rack on the shoulder
The old man follows the road without a word

낙엽에 쓰는 글

멀리 보이는 창문에
물든 노을이 아름다워도
방안에는 어두움이 짙다

질퍽한 운명에 찢긴 잎새
석양에 먼지를 털어내고
씻고 씻어도
회오리가 몰고 오는 회한悔恨을 막을 수 없다

어둑한 방안에 홀로 앉아
지난날에 못다한 사랑의 아쉬움에
말라가는 잎새를 본다

낙엽 위에
석양의 붓으로 쓰고 싶은 글은
'늦가을에 찢긴 행복은 그리움'이라고….

흩날리는 낙엽 위에 신神의 발자국이 찍혀있었다

Writing on Fallen Leaves

Although the glow of the setting sun coloring
The window seen far away is beautiful
The darkness is deep in the room

A leaf torn by a grim destiny
Despite the dust is shaken off at the sunset
And washed over again
The remorse brought by whirlwinds cannot be prevented

Sitting alone in the dim room
With the regret for love that could not be done in the past
I see drying leaves

On the fallen leaves
What I want to write with the brush of the sunset is
“The happiness torn in late autumn is longing"... .

The footprints of God are stamped on the blown leaves.

이슬의 노래

잎 가에 매달려
언제 떨어질지 모르는 이슬방울에서
천진난만한 미소를 보았습니다
잠시 잊었던 주님의 얼굴이었습니다

미래를 걱정 않고 반짝이는 영롱한 빛
내 마음을 한없이 부끄럽게 합니다

잎 사이 숨어 있는 이슬까지 감싸듯
나의 아픔을 보듬어 주는 손길로
맘과 몸을 조심스레 감싸줍니다

에스겔 골짜기에
내 뼈가 흩어져 있다 해도
당신의 생기가 나를 일으킬 때까지
감사와 기도로 노래하렵니다.

Song of Dew

Hanging on the edge of leaves
From the dewdrops that may fall at any moment
I saw an innocent smile
It was the face of the Lord I forgot for a while

The shining brilliant light that shines without worrying about the future
Makes me ashamed beyond measure

As it covers even the dew hiding between the leaves
With a hand that embraces my pain
It carefully embraces my mind and body

In the valley of Ezekiel
Even if my bones are scattered
Until your vitality raises me
I will sing with thanks and prayer.

덧없는 길

안 늙고 싶은데 늙어야 하고
꿈에라도 보고파도 안 꾸이는 꿈
세상에 뜻대로 되는 게 없다

시간이 도는 건지, 내가 도는 건지
어지러운 세상
알 듯 말 듯
내 이름마저 기억이 어슴푸레하다

한 줌도 안 되는 원소로 돌아가는 게
아름다운 건지
두렵고 허무한 건지 해석도 제멋대로다

어디서 와서 어디로 가는지 알면서도
모르는 척
어려운 언어로 논리를 편다

무식한들, 유식한들, 가는 길은 하나
왜 가는지도 모르고 가는 발걸음
남아있는 초췌한 내 모습조차 볼 수가 없다

Evanescent Way

Although I do not want to get old, I have to get old
Although I want to see something even in dreams, I cannot dream as I want
There is nothing that comes up to my expectation in the world

Although I am not sure
Whether time turns or I turn,
The world is dizzy
Even my name is dimly remembered

Whether returning to less than a handful of elements
Is beautiful
Or fearful and futile, the interpretation is arbitrary.

Although they know from whether they came and to where they go
As if they do not know
They set out logical arguments in difficult languages

Whether ignorant or knowledgeable, there is only one way for them to go
They go even without knowing why they go
I cannot even see my remaining haggard figure

번민煩悶의 늪에서

시냇물처럼 범람하던 정열을 사랑하는 이의 가슴에 쏟아붓고
육체의 얄팍한 욕망에 사랑의 노예로 지나온 한 생애
개천이 마르면
원망이 목을 끌어안는다

나는 나를 위한 편협 된 표준을 세운다

나를 이해하지 못하고
괴로움의 도가니에서 건져내지 못하는 신神이라면
이 미약한 믿음의 입으로 원망의 대상이 되기 때문에
어찌 신神이라 부를 수 있을까

루게릭병을 앓듯 노화는 근육을 빠지게 하고
세월이 뼈를 갉아먹을 때
아름다움도 잊고
의지意志도
갈망도 잊고
판별력은 안개에 싸여
혼란과 무료無聊함만 육체를 지배하고 있다

In the Swamp of Anguish

After pouring the passion that was flooding like the water of a stream into the heart of my beloved
My life lived as a slave of love due to the thin desire of the body
When the stream has dried
Resentment hugs my neck

I set a narrow standard for me

Not understanding me
If God cannot rescue me from the crucible of suffering
How can I call him God?
Because he will become the object of resentment by this mouth with weak faith

When aging leads to muscle loss as with suffering from Lou Gehrig's disease
And years gnaw bones
Beauty is forgotten
As well as will
And longing
And discrimination is buried in fog
So that only confusion and boredom dominate the body.

멸망의 빗자루에 쓸려나갈 흙에 기록될 나의 이름

상한 갈대를 꺾지 않고
꺼져가는 등불을 끄지 않는 자여!
마른 땅에 허약한 뿌리를 내린 영혼일지라도
내 혀끝에 달린 가시로
사랑하는 이의 가슴에 상처를 내지 않고
화농할 죄罪의 세균을 퍼트리지 않는
영원한 사랑의 소유자 되기를 원할 뿐이다

My name that will be written on the dirt that will be swept away by the broom of collapse

The one who does not break the bruised reed
And does not extinguish a dying lamp!
Even if he is a soul that put down weak roots in a dry land
I just want him to be the owner of eternal love
Who does not hurt the heart of the beloved,
With thorns on the tip of his tongue
Or spread the germs of sin, that will suppurate

한 송이 구름 되어

떨어질 듯 말 듯
풀 끝에 맺힌 이슬에게
바람은 애증 어린 추억을 들려줍니다

꽃잎보다 여리고 상하기 쉬운 내 마음
시련으로
기쁨으로
걸음마를 떼며
인생을 배우며 성숙하던 때가 추억으로 남습니다

깊은 골짜기에 추억이 안개처럼 서리다가
언어가 필요 없는 오래된 화폭에 잠이 듭니다
가끔, 늙은이에겐
아름다운 형용사나 부사에 의해 낚여져 나오는
케케묵은 사랑이나 슬픔이었을지 몰라도
그 속엔 진실이 살아있습니다

이슬처럼 마르거나 떨어져 가야 하는 운명인데
어찌 사랑이나 슬픔을 완전히 내 것으로
소유할 수 있겠습니까?
잠시 빌려 쓰다 돌려주고 가야 합니다

청명하고 투명한 하늘에
하얀 구름 한 송이 흐르고 있습니다

After Becoming A Cloud

Seeming to fall at any moment
To the dew hanging on the end of the grass
The wind tells memories laden with love and hatred

Those days when my heart softer than petals and tender
With trials
And joys
Taking off baby steps
Was maturing while learning remain as memories

The memories misted up the deep valley like fog
And fall asleep on an old canvas that does not need language
Sometimes, for an old man
Caught by beautiful adjectives or adverbs
The probably outdated love or sadness
Has truth living in it

As the fate is to dry or fall off like dew
How can I have love or sadness
As completely mine?
I have to borrow it for a while and return it when I go.

In the clear and transparent sky
A white cloud is flowing

무력감無力感속에서

희망이 많으면 걱정이 많고
욕망에 허덕이면 만족이 없는 것

얼기설기 얽혀있는 희망과 욕망
이만큼 먼 길 걸어와 뒤돌아보면
불행한 기억이 더 또렷하다

젊음을 불태우며 사랑하는 짝을 찾아
뒤돌아보지 않고 둥지를 빠져나간
한 마리 새

내가 보기에 이국 하늘 아래
구석지고 후미진 곳에서
고생하는 아들 생각
까맣게 잊으려 노력해도
하루도 빠짐없이 선명히 마음을 적시는
사념思念이 나를 괴롭힌다

들이나 산에 피는 메꽃처럼
화려하지도 천賤하지도 않는 순연純然한 자태로
사랑하는 자의 결점도
아름답게 봐야 하는 마음은 뻔하지만
설익은 내 마음은 고난주간이 더욱 씁쓸하다

In the Sense of Helplessness

Those who have many hopes have many worries, and
Those who struggle in desires cannot be satisfied

Hopes and desires are intertwined
When I look back the long way, I have walked thus far
Unfortunate memories are clearer

Burning youth, to find a lover
A bird
That left the nest without looking back

In my view, under the sky of a foreign country
At a place secluded and sequestered
My son is undergoing hardships
Although I make effort to completely forget
Clearly wetting my mind every day
Evil thoughts torment me

Like the flower of convolvulus blooming in fields or mountains
With a pure and natural figure that is neither humble nor splendid
The mind that should regard even the fault of the beloved
As beautiful is obvious
But my unripe heart feels bitter during the Holy Week

떠나보내는 마음

보이지 않을 때까지 손을 흔들며
후회하면서도 보내야 하는 마음이 아프다

참아야 하지만 참지 못하고
지지 않으려고 맞서는 변명
본심이 아닌데도
눈시울을 적시면서 보내야 할 때
결국, 통곡 없이는 넘어설 수가 없다

아버지와 형과 동생
모두가 축복받은 성직자였건만
흙에서 나온 몸 흙으로 돌아가야 하는 짜여진 프로그램에서
부활의 그 날까지 안식할 것을 비는 마음으로
누나와 나만 이 세상에 남았다
한 삽에 정을 담고
또 한 삽에 용서를 비는 마음 담아
취토를 한다

시간이 흐를수록 쌓여가는 이 괴로움
누가 알까 마는
천성天城에서 만나게 될 그날까지
조심스레 나 홀로 길을 가면서
지나온 발자국을 뒤돌아 본다

Mind of Letting You Go

Waving hands until unable to see
I had a broken heart as I have to let you go while regretting

Unable to bear although I had to bear,
I made excuses not to lose
Even though it was not my real intention
When I had to let you go while wetting my eyes
Eventually, I could not pass over without wailing

Father, elder brother, and younger brother
Although all of them were blessed clerics
In the structured program where the bodies that came from dirt should go back to dirt
With a heart to pray for rest until the day of resurrection
Only my sister and I remain in this world.
Putting affection on one shovel
And the mind to bag for forgiveness on another shovel
I take soil

This suffering that builds up as time passes
Who should know, but
Until the day we meet in the heavenly castle
Carefully walking alone
I look back at the past footsteps

갈보리 산의 보혈寶血

수치와 치욕으로 물든 산정에 뱉어놓은 경멸
고문과 채찍으로 뜯긴 살 조각
차마 볼 수 없어
해가 눈을 가릴 때
땅도 진동하며 울고 있었다

'신神의 아들이면 형틀에서 내려오면 될 것을...'
혼자 되뇌는 마음
조롱 아닌 진정한 말이 입가에 맴돌지만
군중에 휩쓸려
진실을 고백하기 어려워 부끄럽기만 하다

아버지가 신神인데 무엇 때문에
인간에게 아들을 내어주었을까?
성전에서 상인들을 쫓아내는 그런 분노로
참을 인忍자에 달궈 낸 화염의 칼로
모조리 베지 않고 스스로가 제물祭物이 되다니

고통과 외로움조차 육신을 떠나
머리의 가시관, 손과 발, 옆구리에는 창에 찔려 흘러나온 피
우리에겐 보혈이 되어
영생의 문으로 인도함이 아니었던가!

Precious Blood on Mount Calvary

The contempt that was spit on the mountaintop stained with shame and humiliation
Since the pieces of flesh torn out by torture and whipping
Could not be endured when seen
When the sun covers the eyes
The ground was crying while shaking

'If he was a son of God, he could come down from the rack...'
I was repeating alone in my mind
True words, not a mockery, lingered around my mouth
But swept by the crowd
It was hard to confess the truth, which is just shameful

Why the father, who is God,
Gave his son to humans?
With the rage to drive merchants out of the church
With a knife of flames heated in the character meaning endurance
He did not cut everybody but became a sacrifice by himself.

Even pain and loneliness left the body
The blood bled due to the crown of thorns on the head and the hands, feet, and sides stabbed by spears
Become precious blood for us
To lead us to the gate of eternal life!

가끔, 비열의 떡을 떼며
죄의 잔을 마시고 후회할 때마다
빈 형틀을 우상처럼 쳐다보는 나의 버릇
혼란스럽지만
당신에 대한 그리움만은 버릴 수가 없다

수천 년 지난 산정에는
시공간을 초월하여 마르지 않는 피가
아직도
내 곁에 흐르고 있다

Every now and then when I pound the rice cake of dastardliness
Whenever I drink a cup of sin and regret
My habit of looking at the empty rack like an idol
Is confusing, but
I cannot throw away my longing for you

Although thousands of years has passed, at the mountaintop,
The blood that does not dry out transcending time and space
Still
Flows by my side

그녀의 부활절

그녀의 얼굴에는
지난날이 서려있다
어둡고 밝은 선線들이 잔잔하게 골을 잡고
우수에 잠긴 슬픔이 눈가에 흐르고 있다

시간에 밀려 떠내려가는 배가 되어
이정표 없이 운명이 가리키는 파도 위에서 배회한다
화려함도 퇴색하고 청바지 뒤 호주머니에 젊음만 집어넣고
파도 위에 노를 젓고 있다

빨래판 같은 삶의 파도 속에서
온 힘을 다해 아래로 밀어내는 생명체
남의 친정어머니들을 보면서 몹시 부러워한다
그녀에겐
몸에서 베여 나온 진한 액체 같은 눈물만 흘렀다
어떤 신화에 나오는 신神에게 질투의 화살에 맞은 몸처럼
차가운 땅속에서
그리운 이의 손길을 기다리며 나날들을 보내는
주인공이라고 말하고 싶은 심정이다
세상이 복잡하거나 슬픈 것이 아니라 그녀의 머리가 복잡하고 슬
퍼졌다

Her Easter

On her face
The past is lingering
Dark and bright lines gently furrow, and
The sorrow immersed in melancholy flows around the eyes.

Became a ship that is carried away by time
She wanders on the waves pointed by the fate without milestones
The splendor faded and with only the youthfulness put into the pocket behind the jeans
She is pulling on the oars on the waves

In the waves of life like a washboard
A life pushing down with all its might
On seeing others' married women's mothers, she envies them very much
On her
Only tears like a thick liquid oozed out from the body flowed.
Like a body shot by an arrow of jealousy from a god appearing in a myth
In the cold ground
Spending days waiting for the hand of the person missed by her
The heroine is what I would like to describe her
Not the world is complicated or sad, but her head became complicated and sad.

거룩한 신神의 계획된 힘에 이끌려
불타지 않은 가시나무 앞에 서서
영원자의 음성을 듣는다
성스러운 이의 손이 그녀의 머리 위에 얹혀졌다
행복감이 전신에 흐르고 기쁨이 마음을 감전시켰다
지난날이 사라지고 새날이 밝았다

부활절 아침이었다

Led by the planned power of the holy deity
Standing in front of an unburned thorn bush
She hears the voice of the eternal one
The hand of the holy one was placed on her head.
A feeling of happiness flows throughout her body, and joy shocked her heart.
The past has gone, and the new day has dawned

It was the Easter morning

봉인封印을 떼다

신神은 조심스레 창문을 열고 밤하늘의 유성을 가리킨다
나는 두 손으로 눈을 감쌌다 아름답게 보이던 것이 두려움으로 변했다 영원에 대한 의문이 생겼다 지옥 외에는 모든 것이 아름답다고 생각했기 때문이다 시인의 서정抒情은 유성처럼 소멸해 가기 시작했다

신神과 사람을 혼란으로 밀어 넣는 괴상한 언어
우한 바이러스19, 펜데믹이라는 말
신神과의 '고강도 사회적 거리 두기'를 시작한다
인간은 시간을 따라 흘러가며 부서져도
끊임없이 머물기를 원하는 패러독스
신神의 진노가 시작된다 봉封해 놓은 여섯 번째의 인印을 뗀다
해는 검은 장례복을 입어 빛을 잃었으며
달이 핏빛으로 변하는 환상을 나에게 보여주었다

창조하고
아름다워 기뻐하고
이처럼 사랑하여 독생자를 보내주고도
왜 밤하늘의 유성처럼 우리를 없애려 하는지!

Removed the Seal

The deity carefully opens the window and points to the shooting star in the night sky.
I covered my eyes with my two hands. What seemed beautiful turned into fear. Questions about eternity arose because I thought everything was beautiful except for hell.

Weird language that pushes God and man into chaos
Wuhan virus 19, the word pandemic
We begin "High-intensity Social Distancing" with God
Although humans flow along time and are broken
A paradox that they want to stay constant
The wrath of God begins. The sixth seal that sealed the wrath is removed.
The sun lost light because it is wearing black funeral clothing
The moon showed me the illusion that its color is turned into blood red.

Despite that after creating
God was delighted as we were beautiful
And sent his the only-begotten Son because he loved us so much
Why he is trying to get rid of us like shooting stars in the night sky!

죄악을 짓기 때문이라고 어릴 적부터 배운 것이 사실이라면
죄악만 없애버리면 될 텐데
머리에 갈등이 생겼다

나는 갈등에도 불구하고 온라인으로 예배를 드렸다

신神은 대답할 가치가 없는 듯 마지막 일곱 번째 봉인封印을 떼려 한다

If it is true that you are removing us because we commit sins
as I learned when I was young
You can just remove sins
Conflicts arose in my head

Despite the conflicts, I held service online

God is about to take off the seventh seemingly because my question is not worthy of answering.

휘어진 시야

세상에 취해버린 눈
어느새 모든 게 휘어져 보인다

하늘에서
영롱한 빛이 내린다
첨탑 위
붉은 눈물 뚝뚝 흘리는
네온사인 십자가
도회지의 헝클어진 빛이 안타깝다

잡雜된 두 눈으로 받는 형벌보다
깨끗한 한 눈으로
영원한 기쁨을 누리고 싶다

왼쪽 눈이 휘어져 보이는 세상
남은 눈 하나로
인생길 험하여 고통이 따라도
환희의 나라 향해 나아가련다

Bent Sight

The eyes intoxicated by the world
Everything looks bent already

From the sky
Brilliant light falls
On the spire
Dripping red tears
Neon sign cross
The tangled light in the downtown area is regrettable

Rather than the punishment received with the wanton two eyes
With one clean eye
I want to enjoy eternal joy

The world where the left eye looks bent
Even though pain follows because the path of life is rugged
With one remaining eye
I will go toward the country of joy

참회懺悔

나는 땅에 떨어진 벼락 몇 개를 주웠다
이별, 죽음, 망각….
두려움과 체념한 언어들의 파편이 너절하다
나의 머리는 슬픔으로 채워지고
보는 것마다 눈물의 근원이 되어
과거가 데스마스크로 남아있다

추억 속에 가두어 둔 후회들이 비밀의 문을 열고
밖으로 나오려 안간힘을 쓴다
별빛, 장미꽃, 낙엽… ,
시간에 흔들리는 수많은 피조물이 도운 사랑인데
혼자서만 앓아야 하는 열병

뇌성을 품은 검은 구름이 걷히고
광풍이 고요 속에 잠들면
분노를 끓게 하는 언어는
영원한 이별을 못 한 채
혓바닥으로 추억을 핥고 있지만
지금은 이별처럼 목멘 차가운 정적만 흐른다
아무에게나 내놓기 싫은 교만스런 독선이
심한 빈혈을 불러들여 온 천지가 하얗다

Penitence

I picked up several thunderbolts that fell to the ground
Parting, death, oblivion... .
Fragments of fear and resigned languages are messy
My head is filled with sadness
Everything I see becomes a source of tears and
The past remains as a death mask

The regrets shut up in memories strain to open the secret door
And come out
Starlight, roses, fallen leaves... ,
The love was helped by countless creations shaken by time
But it is a fever that must be suffered alone

When the black clouds carrying thunder parted
And the gale fell asleep in silence
The language that stirs up anger
Failed to part forever, and
Licks memories with the tongue, but
Now, like parting only choked cold silence flows
The arrogant self-righteousness of not wanting to release to anybody
Summoned severe anemia so that the entire world is white

사망이 창문을 넘어 들어온다 해도
나는
별빛처럼 어둠 속을 뚫고 나오는 추억을
슬픔과 그리움으로 조각彫刻을 구상하고
번민과 고통으로 돌을 쪼아 형태를 만들며
눈물로 조각품彫刻品을 완성시킨다

이것이 참회며 회개다

Even if death comes through the window
I
Conceive a sculpture with sadness and longing from memories
that break through the darkness like starlight
Cut stones into shape with agony and pain, and
Complete the sculpture with tears

This is penitence and repentance

붓꽃으로 다가온 당신
You Who came to Me as an Iris

2021년 1월 05일 인쇄
2021년 1월 11일 발행

지은이 | 최원철
펴낸이 | 박중열
펴낸곳 | 다솜출판사
부산광역시 중구 대청로 135번길 10-1
TEL.(051)462-7207~8 FAX. 465-0646
등록번호 1994년 4월 22일 제2001-000001호

정가 15,000원

ISBN 978-89-5562-677-3 03810